A Short History
of Scene Design
in Great Britain

Drama and Theatre Studies

GENERAL EDITOR: KENNETH RICHARDS
ADVISORY EDITOR: HUGH HUNT

The Theatre of Goethe and Schiller
John Prudhoe

Theatre in the Age of Garrick
Cecil Price

FORTHCOMING

British Theatre, 1950–70
Arnold Hinchliffe

The Irish Theatre
Micheál Ó hAodha

A Short History of Scene Design in Great Britain

SYBIL ROSENFELD

ROWMAN AND LITTLEFIELD
Totowa, New Jersey 07512

First published in the United States 1973
by Rowman and Littlefield, Totowa, New Jersey

ISBN 0-87471-178-9

Library of Congress Cataloging in Publication Data

Rosenfeld, Sybil Marion, 1903–
 A short history of scene design in Great Britain.

 (Drama and theatre studies)
 Bibliography: p.
   1. Theaters—Great Britain—Stage-setting and
scenery. I. Title.
PN2091.S8R59   792'.025'0942   73-1621
ISBN 0-87471-178-9

Filmset and printed in Great Britain by
BAS Printers Ltd, Wallop, Hampshire

Contents

Plates

Author's Note

When, either in the notes or in the text, an author's name only is given, the full reference to the book or article in question will be found in the Book List (pp. 198–205) under the relevant section.

Acknowledgments

The gathering of photographs for this book has necessitated my worrying several people and institutions. In addition to the acknowledgments made to them under the list of plates, I should like to thank the following for all the trouble they took on my behalf: Miss Brooke Barnett, Keeper of the University of Bristol Theatre Collection; Mr. Edward Craig; Dr. Levi Fox O.B.E., Director, and his assistant, Miss Eileen Robinson, of the Shakespeare Centre; Mr. John Goodwin, Press Officer, Royal Shakespeare Theatre, Stratford-upon-Avon; Mr. Terence Gray; Mr. Cecil Lewis; Miss Sheila Porter, Press Officer, Royal Opera House Covent Garden; Mr. David Rutherston; Mr. Gordon Woodruff, University of Birmingham; Mr. Thomas Wragg, Keeper and Librarian, Devonshire Collection, Chatsworth. I am particularly indebted to Mr. John Bury, Mr. Ralph Koltai, Mr. Oliver Messel C.B.E. and Mr. John Piper C.H. for their generosity in supplying photographs of their work.

To Mrs. Christina Gascoigne I owe a debt of gratitude for the fine photographs that she took.

As always the staffs of the Enthoven Collection, Victoria and Albert Museum, and of the British Museum Reading and Print Rooms have been invariably helpful and patient.

Last, but by no means least, I have to express my thanks to Mrs. Ann Merriman for her efficient typing from my difficult handwriting.

SYBIL ROSENFELD

Introduction

The history of scenery in Great Britain from medieval to modern times has not hitherto been written. In international histories of decor British contributions usually, though with one or two exceptions, play only a secondary role and it is one of the purposes of this survey to show that they deserve more consideration than has generally been recognised. The nearest approach to a detailed study of British scenic history is Richard Southern's *Changeable Scenery*, to which all subsequent writers on the subject must be greatly indebted, but the necessary limitation of his subject has meant a confinement to the period from Inigo Jones to the early 20th century and a concentration on technique rather than on design. His book is nonetheless the foundation on which all succeeding work must rest. In addition several general histories of the theatre have short sections on scenery and a good deal of work has been published on a few leading designers such as Inigo Jones and Gordon Craig. More has to be dug out from articles and reviews in late 19th and 20th century periodicals and from catalogues of exhibitions of scene design. I have endeavoured to gather together some of this scattered material.

The history of British scene design may be divided into five main periods. The first of these covers the medieval staging of the miracle plays and moralities. Its main feature was the dispersal of scenic units in the playing place and the simultaneous appearance of these units, each of which was employed in turn as the series of plays or the plot progressed. In this respect scenery followed the pictorial art of the time in which we frequently find succeeding episodes of a saint's life illustrated in a single picture. This type of staging was continued in the masques and progresses of Queen Elizabeth's reign, but the first public theatres broke away from the conception of dispersed scenery to replace it by a great open stage on which successive scenes were played with only a few properties, brought in or discovered as needed and then removed or concealed. Simultaneity had been replaced by succession.

The second period was a sudden revolutionary break which ushered in an entirely new style. Inigo Jones introduced from Italy painted perspective scenery in the early 17th century. Though employed in masques and pastorals at court or in the mansions of the aristocracy, for a theatre narrowly confined to an élite group, he nevertheless established a type of scenery which, after the Restoration, was adopted in public play-houses and has continued in developed forms to our own day. Renaissance art came late to England and, when it came, was apt to be more restrained than in the rest of Europe. We have little to compare with the sumptuous baroque fantasies of continental scenographers; yet because Inigo Jones was a scenic genius, his imaginative inventions and artistry won admiration even from foreign spectators.

It was within this Italianate scenic framework that the next two developments are found. They did not arrive with the same suddenness as the reforms of Jones and they over-lapped considerably with one another. The third period was a breakaway from the formalised Renaissance perspectives to a style which favoured the irregular and the picturesque and was a product of the growth of the romantic movement in which England led the way. Its first leading exponent here was the Alsatian, De Loutherbourg, who was employed by Garrick. Romantic scenery remained one of the dominant characteristics throughout most of the 19th century.

The fourth development was that of realism which had been creeping in, particularly in landscape, during the second half of the 18th century and, in the early 19th, took an archaeological turn in which Capon and J. P. Kemble are associated with attempts to reproduce historically accurate architecture. The flowering of realism came with the productions of Mme Vestris in the 1830's in which she scrupulously xvii reproduced the living rooms of the upper middle class in all their detail. The introduction of the box set led to the substitution of lateral walls and ceiling cloth for interiors for the system of parallel wings and borders which had subsisted from the time of Inigo Jones. The great Shakespearean productions of Charles Kean were unrivalled elsewhere in magnificence of setting and fidelity to archaeological sources and were in themselves romantic. But when realism reached ridiculous and self-defeating lengths at the end of the century the time was ripe for a reaction.

The new stagecraft brought in by Appia and Craig was the fifth and last major shift. It was as revolutionary as that of Inigo Jones, involving an entirely new conception of the function of scenic art and with it a radical change of form, whereas the intervening periods of romantic and realistic settings were the result of changes in taste and so are of a less fundamental nature. Art had pointed the way in futurist and abstract painting to the overthrow of representation. The long hegemony of painted, illusionistic scenery was at an end and it was gradually replaced by plastic and architectural units which symbolised the emotion and mood of the play.

In our own time we are as likely to see sets of this kind as we are to see painted ones. In addition technological advances have influenced staging in such ways as the employment of new materials and multimedia and kinetic elements which mingle with designs based on past periods or with no scenes at all, only the bare brick walls of the theatre itself.

CHAPTER I

Medieval and Tudor Scenic Elements

Medieval Scenes

Medieval scenic units were also three-dimensional and symbolic though in an entirely different mode from the modern. The scenes were isolated from one another, each a world in itself, which appeared simultaneously in the acting area or successively on pageant wagons, each of which bore its own play in a cycle. There was no design relationship and no attempt to create a singleness of impression or overall atmosphere.

In England there were two types of staging: the stationary, in which the cycle of plays was presented in an open space on whose perimeter the scenic units were arranged; and the perambulatory, where pageant wagons, owned and designed by various guilds, processed through a town, each with its separate play. The Lincoln cycle is an example of the first kind and those of York and Chester of the second. Both consisted basically of an open space or *platea* in which the actors played and a set of scenic houses or *loci* built on scaffolds or wagons. No English picture exists of either and we have to depend on descriptions, property lists and two French illuminated manuscripts, Fouquet's miniature of the martyrdom of Saint Apollonia, *c.* 1400, and Cailleau's of the

Valenciennes Passion Play, 1547.[1] Both represent the stationary type, since the processional was hardly known on the Continent. In the first the houses are arranged in a semi-circle on scaffolds, interspersed with others for privileged spectators. In the second they are aligned in a row, except for a ship and hell, which are further forward, and are more sophisticated in style with painted backings.

Three English plans show that they were sometimes presented in a circular place. The Cornish mystery cycle known as the *Ordinalia*[2] was probably produced in one of the pre-historic Cornish rounds and had eight scaffolds on the perimeter; the Cornish *Life of Saint Meriasek* had thirteen; the later morality play, *The Castle of Perseverance*,[3] about 1425, had five scaffolds—for God, the world, the flesh and the devil at the four points of the compass and a fifth for Covetousness—with a castle for Mankind in the centre, which was on stilts and could be ascended by the actors. The number of houses varied and in the Digby *Mary Magdalen* plays there were as many as sixteen. They were constructed of wooden frames covered with canvas and could accommodate several actors, who waited their turn to descend by ladder or ramp to the *platea* below and returned when their play was finished. A certain amount of painting was used but the settings were primarily built up. They represented temples, houses or palaces of such characters as Pilate and Herod, often furnished with a throne or 'state'; also mountains (for Calvary), ships (for Noah), trees (for Eden), castles (for Jerusalem) and, most important, heaven on the stage right and hell on the left symbolically placed. When one or other of these units was activated this represented a change of scene and some had curtains which could be opened and closed. The heavens were

1. Reproduced in Wickham, Vol. 1.
2. Revived in the Perran Round by Bristol University Drama Department, 1969. The cycle took three days.
3. N. Crohn Schmitt has argued that this was not performed in the round. 'Was There a Medieval Theatre in the Round?', *Theatre Notebook*, July, October 1969, Vol. 23, pp. 130–142; Vol. 24, pp. 18–25.

supplied with clouds, hell was represented by a monster's gaping mouth, and Noah's Ark by a ship. Such iconographical symbols are paralleled in church carving[4] and in illuminated manuscripts.

Guild pageant wagons used similar types of setting. Their bases were often wrapped round with painted cloths and they bore a superstructure of two storeys, the lower being used as a tiring room for the actors, or serving for hell mouth, the upper for the performance. Since this acting area was rather restricted, a scene was sometimes played in the street below, as in the famous instance of Herod raging. There may also have been platforms attached to the wagons to give additional playing space.

Mechanical effects were used, the oldest of which was the moving star which guided the magi; the most common, ascents and descents operated by ropes and a windlass, and traps. Painted cloud work concealed the ropes by which Christ ascended in the Chester cycle and angels descended from the heavens. Fire played its part when a cloud descended and set a temple alight, or when a burning altar was shown in *Cain and Abel*, and fire crackers regularly issued from hell mouths. A link to set the world on fire cost 5d!

Scenic elements parallel to those of the plays are to be found in tournaments and street theatres, and for them we have more illustrations. Professors Kernodle and Wickham have been pioneers in examining these rewarding fields and have helped us to visualise the scenic devices which they shared with the miracle stages. Tilts were frequently incorporated into quasi-dramatic fables of knights storming symbolic castles and rescuing or conquering the ladies within. Castles were painted set pieces and each knight entered in his chariot, which might represent a ship riding on a sea of painted cloth, or a green hill on which were painted trees and roaming beasts such as were also found in the miracles. Other devices

---

4. See M. D. Anderson, *Drama and Imagery in English Medieval Churches*, 1963.

were gateways, pavilions, fountains and trees with painted leaves and flowers behung with armorial bearings. Tournaments or barriers, as they were sometimes called, were staged well into the 17th century, when two of them were devised by Ben Jonson and Inigo Jones, who were responsible for the masques.

Street theatres were set up from the early 13th century to the time of Charles II on the processional routes of coronations, royal nuptials, civic welcomes and the like occasions. They took the form of triumphal arches, gateways and castles from which stages projected for the presentation of *tableaux vivants* or eulogistic orations. In addition to special constructions, existing city gateways, market crosses and water-conduits were decorated to serve as stations where the processions halted. Thus Temple Bar was adorned as a forest for St. John the Baptist at the entry of Richard II, whilst at that monarch's coronation in 1377 a castle with four towers was erected in Cheapside from which maidens scattered golden leaves and imitation golden florins. By 1501 upper and lower stages were introduced and these two-storeyed erections became customary in the 16th century, enabling ascents and descents to be engineered by means of windlass machinery and traps. For Edward VI a double scaffold was hung with silks and cloth of gold; in the heavens were depicted sun and stars on clouds of white sarsenet from out of which a phoenix descended to the lower scaffold, where it settled on a mountain and scattered symbolic white and red roses. Similar, though probably less rich, effects must have been seen in the miracle plays watched by the same spectators in the streets who would expect no less from a religious than from a secular pageant.

Foreign artists such as Holbein and Hans Eworth were commissioned to design these street theatres. Those devised by Jonson and Dekker for the entry into London of James I[5] anticipated effects used in the masques, such as a globe turned by the four elements and filled with figures and, more signifi-

4 5. Engraved by Willem Kip after Stephen Harrison.

cantly, an arch adorned with a perspective of the houses, towers and steeples of London presumably painted, and the first perspective we know of in any theatre here.

All the entertainments so far mentioned were held in the open air by daylight, but a parallel development took place in halls by candlelight often in association with banquets. The most important scenically were the disguisings, a mixture of masquerade, music, dancing and spectacle, and their successors, the masques. Henry VIII was addicted to such festivities, in which he participated as a masquer. Familiar scenic items appeared in these shows. At the wedding of Prince Arthur and Katharine of Aragon in 1501 at Westminster Hall were exhibited a castle drawn on by artificial beasts which held ladies and singers, a pageant ship bearing Hope and Desire, a mount of love from which the knights assaulted the castle, a tabernacle and an arbour. At an entertainment given to the French Ambassadors at Greenwich in 1528 a curtain was used to conceal a mountain adorned with roses and pomegranates for the men masquers, whilst the ladies issued out of a cave. These pieces were either dispersed on the hall floor or brought in on cars, as for some miracle cycles; only the disposal of the audience was different—the monarch occupying one end and the rest being seated on raised tiers along the sides of the hall. Medieval elements and conventions thus continued into the Tudor period.

Elizabethan Scenes

The accounts of the Master of the Revels provide us with some information about the staging of Elizabethan masques.[6] The only pictorial record is part of a painting in the National Portrait Gallery of Sir Henry Unton's wedding festivity, which does not depict scenery but only fancifully costumed dancers, preceded by children bearing torches, ascending to a raised stage.

6. H. Feuillerat, *Documents Relating to the Office of the Revels in the Time of Elizabeth*, 1908.

Entertainments presented before the Queen at Christmas and Shrovetide, whether plays or masques, used similar scenic elements to those of the disguisings. Carpenters were employed to construct wooden frames which were covered in canvas and painted. An Emperor's palace, a rock and a practicable hill were seen in *A Masque of Hunters and Nine Muses* in 1575. The muses were concealed and then revealed by a veil of sarsenet. The six small cities and three battlements for which payment was made to William Lyzard in 1580 may, however, have represented a departure from the three-dimensional, in which the cities were painted backgrounds to the battlements. A similar combination may be seen in the arch of London already mentioned, at King James's coronation in 1604. Since the Master of the Revels had to be qualified in rudiments of perspective as well as architecture, it seems likely that such city cloths were painted according to the principles of perspective. A list of properties included mountains, forests, beasts, serpents and artificial plants and flowers usually fashioned of silk. The animals of wire and canvas were familiar in the street theatres, but there were also figures of people cut out in wood which could be pulled across the floor, as Serlio had described. The kind of dispersed scenery used is illustrated in the account of an entertainment given to the Queen at Elvetham in 1591 (Plate 1)[7] in which, on an artificial pond, crescent-shaped in symbolic reference to Cynthia, are seen a pinnace, a castle or fort, an island and a snail mount of spiralled hedges which sprouted horns of burning wildfire.

When Elizabeth visited the universities on her progresses the layout was quite different. For classical and other plays special stages were erected at one end of the hall on which the performance took place and the Queen was enthroned. The scenic elements were concentrated on a stage and not dispersed throughout the hall. According to neo-classical prece-

7. John Nichols, *The Progresses and Public Processions of Queen Elizabeth*, 1788, from a contemporary pamphlet.

PLATE I. Dispersed scenery in the entertainment of Queen Elizabeth at Elvetham.

dent for performances of Roman comedies, houses or palaces were placed on both sides of the stage, but these could not have been arranged in perspective, as Professor Wickham has pointed out, since the Queen was seated too close for any vanishing point. At Oxford walls of golden panels and roof were transformed to simulate a Roman palace, an attempt at neo-classical architecture such as might be expected from university authorities affected by Renaissance ideas.[8] Three years previously John Shute's *First and Chief Grounds of Architecture*, the first English book on the principles of Vitruvius, had been printed. Other English scholars were contributing to the knowledge of neo-classical rules, such as Dr. John Dee of Cambridge, who had invented a flying machine for a

8. Wickham, Vol. 1, Appendix H; a translation from John Bereblock's Latin description.

performance of *Pax* in 1546, and had cited Vitruvius in illustration of the principles of architectural proportion. His theories and those of Robert Fludd probably complemented Italian influences on Inigo Jones. The study of optics and mathematics paved the way for the introduction of perspective scenery on the English stage.[9]

After the miracle plays had been suppressed by Protestant enactments in the 1570s, the court became the chief purveyor of scenery until the closing of the theatres in 1642, in spite of the opening of the first public theatre by Burbage in 1576 and the subsequent erection of several playhouses. The professional companies which occupied them were, however, preoccupied by plays and acting rather than by spectacle. Their architectural tiring-houses and great thrust stages could accommodate only a minimum of scenery and machinery. Nor did they need them. Their flexible form of stage enabled them to present constantly shifting scene locations without much more than the tiring house façade provided and their dramatists were poets who revelled in descriptions of places where the action was set. Many scenic units would have been in the way of actors and audience, who surrounded the stage on three sides. So well adapted were the theatres to their purpose that when the Globe and Fortune were rebuilt in the 17th century it was in the old style without provision for perspective scenery by then in use at court.

Nearly all the action took place on the open stage or the upper balcony, the two levels being reminiscent of the two-tiered street theatres. The use of the open platform for different and successive locations had been hinted at in the University performances, whereas the masques still kept to the multiple and dispersed scenic units. Elements of scenery mentioned by Henslowe in his inventory of 1598[10] and in the stage directions of plays prove that the medieval tradition lingered on. These included hell mouth, a rock, three kinds of trees, a moss bank

9. Frances Yates, *Theatre of the World*, 1969.
10. Cited by Wickham, Vol. 2, pp. 310–323, and Hodges, p. 73.

and such properties as a dragon for Faustus, a statue, a chariot and tombs. A few items, such as a cage, steeples, a beacon, a pair of stairs and a heifer for Phaeton, are novel. The city of Rome may have been a gateway such as that of Jerusalem in the Valenciennes Passion Play, but, even if infrequently, painted cloths were in use as in one of the Sun and the Moon. Two tents on opposite sides of the stage must have been occupied by Richard and Richmond but houses were occasionally adjacent. The walls and battlements required for Shakespeare's historical plays may have been scenic structures but probably the balcony was also utilised. As for machinery, there were traps for apparitions, devils and possibly props, and windlass machinery above for descents from heaven, both by individuals and by gods in chairs. Thus Juno descended in the masque scene of *The Tempest*, Hecate flew aloft in *Macbeth* and Jupiter came down mounted on an eagle in *Cymbeline*.

Renaissance elements were certainly introduced into the Elizabethan theatres. At the Swan classical columns, fashioned of wood painted to simulate marble, are shown in a copy of a drawing of the theatre by a Flemish visitor, Johannes de Witt, which was discovered in 1888. In an accompanying description de Witt marked resemblances to the ancient Roman theatre, and Thomas Nashe even considered our stage 'more stately furnished' than the Roman. There is evidence that the theatres were both stately and richly adorned. Coryat, who visited the Venetian theatres in 1611, found that they could not compare with ours. In the penthouse, over the stage, the heavens in some playhouses were painted with clouds, stars and signs of the Zodiac. The arras or tapestry curtain, which hung in front of the tiring house entrance and which could be opened to reveal actors in a back alcove, doubtless added more colour to the stage. What the public theatres contributed were not the scenic entities, which were inherited from the medieval, but a sense of the unity of the playing space and its intimate relationship with the surrounding spectators. Not until the revival of this open stage in our own century was it

9

realised what flexibility had been forfeited by the adoption of the Italian painted perspective scenery.

The individual pieces which persisted for two centuries on English stages lacked any artistic cohesion. The Renaissance setting, when it superseded the medieval, achieved it. But in England the reformation arrested developments which had taken place on the Continent. We have seen that in the revival of classical plays and in some forms of decoration the Renaissance started to seep through, but fear of popery and Spanish power ensured that traditional English staging lingered in all forms of entertainment until a Stuart monarch was enthroned. Then occurred the most fundamental scenic revolution.

CHAPTER II

Inigo Jones and Perspective Scenery

Neo-classical and Italian Forerunners

The Renaissance was based on the rediscovery of the classical arts and sciences. From the point of view of the theatre, the pioneer work was the *De Architectura* of Vitruvius, first published in Rome in 1486 and thereafter in many editions with commentaries and plans as well as translations.[11] Vitruvius was the chief source of information about Greek and Roman theatres and also dealt, not altogether accurately, with their scenes and machines. He described how within the three doors of the Greek *frons scenae* or proscenium were placed three-sided, painted prisms called *periaktoi* which revolved and so changed the scene. There were three types of scene: the tragic, on which the appurtenances of palaces, such as columns, pediments and statues were delineated; the comic, with houses of ordinary citizens and their windows and balconies; and the satyric for rustic humours, whereon were represented landscapes of mountains, woods and caverns. Furthermore, he described the painting of these scenes in perspective as well as machines which were revolved by heavy weights and lesser engines which could be worked by one man. Perspective and machinery were thus associated with the staging of classics.

11. First English translation, 1692.

Actual perspective scenery was used in Ferrara in 1508 by Pellegrino da Udine and in Urbino in 1513 when *La Calandria* was produced with scenes by Giralamo Genga. The scenes were not painted in the flat but modelled in relief. Later that year Baldassare Peruzzi, who had studied Vitruvius, staged *La Calandria* in Rome with scenes and machines, and by 1531 had designed a perspective street. These represented a break-away from the classics, mainly due to the fact that performances were no longer in the open air amphitheatres of classical times but in rectangular palace halls. It was impossible to construct a high proscenium large enough to accommodate the three entrances with their *periaktoi* in such surroundings. The presentation was geared to a prince and his court and not to a great congregation of citizens; the prince had to be placed in an advantageous central position for the perspectives; the rest were seated along the sides of the hall as they were in the Elizabethan masques. Italian designers, intoxicated by the art and science of perspective painting, solved the problem by inventing the single scene, set at the end of the hall opposite the prince on a raised stage. We are indebted to these early artists for the long enduring shape of scenery to come, but their contribution was eclipsed by that of the architect and theorist, Sebastiano Serlio, who exercised the most far-reaching influence on scene design throughout Europe.

Serlio studied under Peruzzi and helped him to investigate and measure classical remains. In 1545 he published the book of his *Architettura* which covers perspective and includes a brief section on the design of theatres and scenography.[12] Here he set out the principles of perspective scenery behind the experiments of Genga and Peruzzi and laid down detailed instructions for their realisation with plans of the theatre, stage, scenery and lighting. His auditorium retains the classical amphitheatre form. The forepart of the stage was level to

12. First English translation, 1611. *The Renaissance Stage*, ed. Barnard Hewitt, 1958, for a modern text.

accommodate dancers, then sloped up to enable the perspectives to be seen. The vanishing point was behind the back wall so as to avoid the impression of houses running into one another and the perspective was emphasised by marking out the floor in diminishing squares.

Serlio made scaled models from which the back scenes were enlarged on flat frames and front scenes on angled frames, one side facing the audience and the other the line of the street. They were backed by a shutter or cloth painted in further perspective. Such superstructures as chimneys and belfries were fashioned of profiled board, whilst projecting features, such as balconies or loggias, were cut out on painted pieces of wood, through which other houses would be glimpsed. Following Vitruvius, Serlio illustrated the three neo-classical scenes and these three designs were the prototypes on which Inigo Jones based his masque scenery (Plate 2, cf. Plate 4).

Lighting was from a central chandelier but shadows were painted as though from a light on one side. Roundels and windows were made of transparent materials with lights placed behind. Glass containers with coloured water, or even wine, were fastened on battens at the backs of the houses, reflecting different tints. Serlio also describes such effects as causing heavenly bodies to pass through the air by wire and thread, and making stage thunder and lightning.

The actor could not have been involved in the scenery to any extent. The difficulty was that he would have looked like a giant upstage amidst the vanishing perspective but would have diminished in size in relation to his surroundings as he came forward. Rather scenery was conceived of merely as a background to the action which took place in front of it on the level forestage.

The first permanent theatre, the Teatro Olimpico, was built by Palladio and Scamozzi in Vicenza, 1580–1584, for an academic society, and is still standing. The type of Roman theatre on which it is based can be seen in Orange. It was a throwback from the work of Serlio in that it reverted to the

PLATE 2. Sebastiano Serlio, satyric scene from *Della Architettura*.

architectural, neo-classical proscenium with a façade pierced by one large central arch and two lesser side openings, to which were added two more at right angles, thus providing five scene areas. It was Scamozzi who, in 1585, filled these with perspective streets constructed of wood and stucco on steep rakes. He thus departed from the Vitruvian *periaktoi*, replacing them by built-up scenery. Because the theatre was

14

designed not for a prince but a learned association, it was necessary for all the spectators in the amphitheatre to see at least one perspective. The system was a dead-end because the scenery could never be changed being imprisoned in the façade openings.

Inigo Jones visited this theatre and has left us a desciption of it as well as some drawings.[13] He mentions that all the houses were in relief, the columns were flat but rounded at the edges, the statues were of marble and imitation bronze 'thos in shortning ar flatt but of hole Releave' (a curiously contradictory phrase) which showed strangely near but well at a distance. The lights were placed at the sides, the floor was painted to resemble pavement, and cornices were made of slanting deal boarding slightly painted. The roof was covered with canvas but there were no clouds.

In his copy of Palladio Jones has sketched a theatre in which he has enlarged the central arch to enclose one wide perspective street instead of five. Scamozzi had already found this solution for the little theatre he built at Sabbioneta, 1588–1590, since the site was too narrow for more than one perspective.

The hold that the Teatro Olimpico had on Jones is testified to by his rebuilding of the Cockpit-in-Court in 1630, which is a strange reversion to a Palladium proscenium with an enlarged central arch and four openings.[14] Three of his designs, for a palace, an army and a prison, fit the measurements of this round-headed arch and must have been for this theatre, but they were painted rather than built-up perspectives.

13. For full text see W. G. Keith, 'A Theatre Project', *Burlington Magazine*, 1917. Jones's copy of Palladio in Worcester College Library has been issued in facsimile by the Oriel Press.
14. Discovered by Hamilton Bell, 'Contributions to the History of the English Playhouse', *Architectural Record*, 1913. W. G. Keith contended that the drawing was by Webb: 'John Webb and the Court Theatre of Charles II', *Architectural Review*, February 1925, but this has been disproved by Bentley, Vol. 6, 274 n. See also R. F. Rowan, 'The Cockpit-in-Court', *The Elizabethan Theatre*, ed. D. Galloway, 1969; Glynne Wickham, *Shakespeare's Dramatic Heritage*, 1969, pp. 151–162.

The great Florentine fêtes, staged to celebrate two Medici weddings in 1586 and 1589, established the full panoply of baroque changeable scenery on the stage. Buontalenti's engraved settings for 1589 became widely distributed and influenced the development of scenery in other countries.[15] There can be little doubt that they were known to Jones, who enjoyed poring over Italian prints and pictures. Both text and illustrations bear witness to the astounding advance that had been made since Serlio's three static scenes of forty years previously. There was a great expansion in the subject matter of the scenes and this was made possible by the invention of machinery for changing them. The mastery of machinery also enabled Buontalenti to present spectacles undreamt of before and to achieve marvellous effects with aerial flyings, sinkings and scene openings. At both festivities a play was acted which, according to classical tradition, had to observe the unity of place in a single scene. But the acts were interspersed with *intermezzi*, which had no such restriction, and in which the taste for spectacular staging could be indulged.

For the fête of 1589 a special stage was constructed in the Uffizi Palace. This was partially framed with gigantic statues of river gods. A red curtain was dropped to reveal another with a painted architectural prospect, which gave place in turn to a view of Rome in which ancient buildings mingled with modern. The comedy of *La Pellegrina* was set in Pisa and there were three perspective streets with triple vanishing points, an effect which had been invented thirty years previously by Salviati, as can be seen by two of his designs in the British Museum. Buontalenti improved on his predecessor by using a combination of a straight axis line in the centre and outward curving ones at the sides to give a less rigid effect. For his seven scene changes Buontalenti probably employed, not full sets of wings and shutters, but the *periaktoi* on which new views were affixed on the sections turned away from the

15. Reproduced with descriptions in A. M. Nagler, *Theatre Festivals of the Medici, 1539–1637*, 1964.

audience. The six other scenes, in addition to Pisa, were of a cloud which opened whilst others rose over a Doric temple downstage; a garden decorated with flowers and animals with a mountain which rose from a trap and had grottoes which themselves opened; a sylvan glade; an inferno into which a fiery sphere descended and opened to reveal the city of Dis and flaming rocks; a sea with reefs on which Amphitrite appeared in a mother-of-pearl shell and pasteboard ships moved in grooves; a final cloud scene with the heavens opening again and five clouds descending whilst two hovered above.

These scenes formed the staple repertory of baroque spectacle throughout Europe and all were adapted by Jones. The machines 'became the model from which the artificers of the whole of Europe took their ideas'. A new international style had been born.

Early Masques

Queen Elizabeth had been economical in her entertainments, but James I was prepared to spend lavishly. During his reign and that of Charles I England caught up on her half century time lag in scenic development and was freed from the isolation which followed the Reformation. This spectacular advance was due to the genius of Inigo Jones, who became responsible for Court entertainments. He visited Italy at least twice and brought to England the illusionist perspective scenery and the baroque style which rendered the Court stage the equal of those of the Continent.

The staging of the masques has been analysed in detail by Professor Allardyce Nicoll, so that we shall need only to describe selected examples to indicate the developments that took place over thirty years.

In his first masque, Daniel's *Vision of Twelve Goddesses*, Hampton Court, 1604, Jones retained the Elizabethan dispersed scenes. The three units were a practicable mount at the lower end of the hall, down which graces and goddesses

17

descended preceded by torch-bearers, as in the Unton masque, and in the concaves of which appeared satyrs; the Cave of Sleep; and Sibylla's Temple with a curtain which dropped to reveal the tableau of a sacrifice. The theme was classical and the presentation simple.

The first of the great series of masques in which Jones collaborated with Ben Jonson was *The Masque of Blackness*, Twelfth Night, 1605. It was the first in which he introduced perspective scenery, though he had used *periaktoi* on a Serlian raked stage earlier in the year for performances at Oxford on the occasion of a royal visit. As in Italy, perspective scenery was designed for the central position of a monarch or important personage, who alone had full benefit from the vistas. He sat in state at the opposite end of the hall from the stage on a level with the horizon line, so that the perspectives 'caught the eye afar off with a wandering beauty'. Guests on the sides had but a wry view of them. Masques were symbolic entertainments in adulation of the virtues of the sovereign or, in the case of wedding masques, of the noble married couple. Poetry, dancing, music and scenery were in collaboration to this end. Courtiers and court ladies in magnificent and fantastic costumes participated as masquers and were revealed in all their glory in some shell grotto or cloud before they descended to dance together and finally to take out members of the audience for further measures.

The *Masque of Blackness* was so called because Queen Anne of Denmark wished to appear with her court ladies as negresses. It opened with a painted curtain depicting a landscape of woods with hunters. When this fell it revealed a seascape in which waves appeared to move and break; Tritons, mermaids and life-size sea horses, bearing Oceanus and Niger, rode on the waters. The motion of the sea horses was controlled by 'a great machine', though one spectator sourly remarked: 'The indecorum was, that there was all fish and no water'. By means of perspective illusion the sea shot down towards the front. The twelve masquers appeared in a concave shell illuminated with a chevron of lights which moved on the sea accompanied by six sea monsters. These carried twelve torch bearers who threw light on the rich silks of the costumes. Sabbatini, writing thirty years later but referring to traditional practice, describes three methods of constructing a sea: by a loose cloth over a frame; by profiled ground rows worked from below, and by cylinders rotated from the sides. Spaces were left between each row of waves to enable boats or shells to pass through. No masking is mentioned, but possibly wings of reefs were installed as in the seascape of the Florentine Festival to which Jones's bears a remarkable resemblance. The sea was backed by a cloudy nightpiece and a personified Moon in white and silver was later discovered on a throne in the upper part of the house crowned with a sphere of light which illumined the clouds. The heaven was vaulted with blue silk set with silver stars. When the Tritons sounded the masquers stepped from their shell to dance on shore and, after they had done so, returned to their shell to echoing songs. Nothing like this had been seen before on the British stage. It was the first unified picture, the first single effect. Motion, light and the brilliant hues of the costumes contributed to the beauty of the scene. Yet it was only a beginning; there was no scene change, no proscenium frame, and no shutters which opened and closed.

The first step towards the proscenium, so necessary for masking, was in *Hymenaei*, a wedding masque of 1606, where two golden statues at each side of the stage were linked by a curtain hung from the roof. In *Hue and Cry After Cupid*, 1608, the proscenium sides were decorated by pilasters supporting statues of Triumph and Victory twice life size, and in *Tethys' Festival*, 1610, by giant gilded figures of Neptune and Nereus with a frieze.

The neo-classic device of the *scena versatilis*, which swivelled to show another scene on the obverse, was used in *Hymenaei*, a convex revolving globe being pivoted to reveal eight masquers on the concave side. The ladies descended in two concave clouds, not perpendicularly 'like a bucket into a well' but sloping gently. Jones experimented with other methods of changing scenes. In the *Lords' Masque*, 1607, a curtain was vertically divided; half was drawn to show a Bower of Flora; the other half a hill. The other neo-classic method of changing scenery was the *scena ductilis*, by which a shutter, divided in the middle, was drawn off to reveal another scene behind. Jones seems first to have employed it in *Hue and Cry After Cupid*, and it soon became the prevalent type. Jones at this time probably used mainly *periaktoi*, but it is not always possible to tell when shutters had replaced them as they certainly had in *Oberon*, 1611, where the whole palace 'opened'.

The Masque of Beauty, 1608, probably not by Jones, used traps for trees to sink, divide in three and disgorge masquers from their tops. A complicated piece of machinery enabled an island, a throne and steps to be revolved in different directions and finally shot forward to the front, perhaps on a wagon. Even the Venetian Ambassador was impressed: 'The cunning of the stage machinery was a miracle, the abundance and beauty of the lights immense'. Something of the effect of myriad, shimmering candlelights is evident in a drawing of *The Masque of Queens*, 1609, in which friezes were filled with coloured lights shining like jewels through bottles filled with tinted liquids. This masque was the first to introduce the anti-masque or grotesque interlude which became a regular feature. Antic actors garbed as hags and devils in hell contrasted vividly with the splendid habits and stately dances of the masquers.

Jones visited Paris in 1609 and absorbed Italian influences through a French medium, as Betterton and Garrick were to do after him. *Tethys' Festival*, 1610, which celebrated the creation of Prince Henry as Prince of Wales, had two scene changes, one of which was accompanied, not only by the customary music, but the descent of three revolving circles of lights and glasses. The music helped to smother the noise of the machinery and the lights to distract attention. The changes may have been part of the marvels, as Dr. Southern believes, but Jones was at pains to provide methods of distraction or concealment in order to make the impact of revelation, particularly of the masquers, more dramatic. For the first time we hear of 'relief' in this masque in the shape of pillars of 'whole round' and ornaments in relief as well as two large figures over the rustic frontispiece. The first relief scene was in Campion's sumptuous *Lords' Masque*, 1613. The stage was divided horizontally, each part being concealed by a curtain. The lower first fell to discover a perspective wood, 'the innermost part being of relief or whole round', the rest painted. This clearly means that the front wings were painted in two dimensions, but on a further inner stage the scenes were modelled to emphasise the more distant part of the perspective. Dr. Southern objects to this interpretation on grounds of artistic inconsistency and the absence of three-dimensional indications in later plans which, however, are for another masquing house. It is true that Jones in his description of the Teatro Olimpico used the word 'relief' in contradictory senses, but it is difficult to deny his specific distinction between relief and painting. Dr. Southern defines relief scenes as cut out profiles against a background placed on the back stage; my own solution is that they were at first modelled and later, when they became a regular feature, were modified to two-dimensional forms but retained the original name. The two-storeyed stage was also an innovation already seen in the street theatres, and used well into the 18th century. It enabled more partial scene changes to be made with increased revelations, and provided practical heavens in which perspectives of clouds with seated deities could be displayed. Thus in the *Lords' Masque* clouds were changed to fires and lights above, a wood was changed to statues below and, finally, the whole scene was unified in a perspective of porticoes. In order to cover both levels of change a transparent cloud was advanced from the side reaching from heavens to earth from which the masquers descended.

21

The wedding of Princess Elizabeth and the Elector Palatine triggered off a set of masques in which a rock, nearly as high as the house, was exhibited. Like the island in *Queens*, it was probably on a truck as it moved forward and broke into two stages of a cloud and a gold mine.

During the time when Jones was in Italy, 1613–1614, the masque for the marriage of the Duke of Somerset was entrusted to an Italian, Constantino de Servi, but was not a success. The *Masque of Flowers* for the same occasion, by an unknown designer, provides us with measurements which are evidence of the large scale of scenery employed. At the further end of the stage was a mount surmounted by a practicable arbour, 33 ft. long and 21 ft. wide, in which the masquers sat concealed by a painted bank of flowers which sank to discover them. They descended to the garden alleys below and met to dance on the forestage. Sir Francis Bacon bore the full expenses of this masque, which amounted to £2,000, an indication of the costliness of these court toys.

Another designer was employed for *Lovers Made Men*, 1617. He was Nicholas Lanier, a French composer and musician, whose scenery was not, however, remarkable. He used a proscenium triumphal arch through which was seen Charon's barque with a perspective of myrtle grove behind. This masque has claims to be the first English opera as it was sung in recitative throughout. In twelve years masques had graduated from a single scene to the presentation of several changes by various methods and from one stage to three different locations, above, below, and in the recess behind. The proscenium arch had been introduced, which provided easier masking, and more complicated machinery had been installed for effects of motion.

Later Masques and Plays at Court

Inigo Jones's new Banqueting House, which still stands, was opened in 1622 with *The Masque of Augurs*. It was equipped with greater facilities for machinery, especially for large traps through which whole scenes could rise from under the stage, as earth rose in this masque. Of the three cloud machines, the central one would accommodate at least five people.

From this time on many more designs for scenery are extant which can be associated with specific pieces. Thanks to the magnificent Chatsworth Collection of drawings by Jones and Webb for masques and plays, these early 17th century entertainments are better illustrated than any others before the 19th century.

After the death of James I in 1625, masques were not only continued under Charles I but were supplemented by pastorals. The first of these was Racan's *L'Artenice* performed by the Queen and her ladies at Somerset House.[16] Jones's designs for the proscenium with draped side curtains and for the single 'standing' scene are extant. The latter is a strange mingling of a village of thatched cottages with a classical portico, and of a distant church with ruins.

The last two masques on which Jonson and Jones collaborated, *Love's Triumph Through Persepolis* and *Chloridia*, both date from 1631. The latter was one of the most elaborate. We have sketches for the first landscape scene, consisting of four pairs of rock wings topped by trees with a back scene of hills and waterfalls and a serene sky above. Jones was to employ this type of landscape with increasing frequency. It had a particularly English atmosphere, especially when distant villages, thatched cottages and cornfields were depicted. There was a local feeling about the designs which can hardly be paralleled in the more formal alleys of Continental scenographers. The sky with transparent clouds was succeeded by a tempest and then by a calm, whilst behind the masking clouds the scene was changed to a bower of goldsmith's work with a rainbow in the sky beyond. The 'further Prospect' changed to air over a low landscape in part covered with clouds. The heavens opened to reveal goddesses and aery

16. Identified by Wm. A. Jackson, 'Racan's L'Artenice', *Harvard Library Bulletin*, Vol. 14.

spirits, whilst from below a practicable hill arose surmounted by a globe with Fame standing on top, and four persons seated on the hill. Fame later mounted on wings whilst the hill sank and the heavens closed. The masque was accompanied by a series of visual changes which kept the eyes of the spectators well occupied.

Jonson had become increasingly restive about the usurpation of the poet's function, which he regarded as the soul of the masque, by that of the decorator which was its ephemeral body. He bitterly resented that Jones had now become the ascendant partner and in protest placed his name before Jones's as the inventors, at which Jones took umbrage. Jonson expressed his indignation in a poem, 'The Expostulation', in which he attacked Jones as a jumped-up architect with a false show of learning and the taste of the audience who:

> doe cry up the Machines and the showes,
> The Majesty of Juno in the cloudes
> And peering forth of Iris in the shroudes . . .
> O showes, showes, mighty showes!
> The eloquence of Masques! What need of prose
> Or verse, or sense, t'express immortal you.

So starts the long controversy that was to bedevil staging for nearly three centuries. Henceforward attacks on the supremacy of spectacle and on its claims for attention over the contribution of the dramatist were frequent. Gordon Craig was to make more far-reaching claims than Jones for the hegemony of the designer, and only in recent years has the tug-of-war come to an end. The two geniuses who had raised the masque to a splendid art form in which poet and painter collaborated could never again work together. Lesser poets were engaged and, though the masques became increasingly more magnificent and varied visually, the balance was impaired and the artistic entity suffered.

There are signs that Jones's invention was also flagging. He began to reproduce designs of the Italian scenographers,

Giulio and Alfonso Parigi, who in turn derived their ideas from Buontalenti's Florentine festivals. In particular, Jones drew on the *intermezzi* scenes of *Il Giudizio di Paride*, which Giulio had designed for a fête in 1608 and which were available in engravings. *Albion's Triumph* by Townsend, 1632, had a Roman setting with scenes of an atrium, forum and amphitheatre, the atrium being adapted from the Temple of Peace in Parigi's sixth *intermezzo*. In *Tempe Restor'd* of the same year the first scene of two-storeyed arbours enriched with statues and branches of trees and surmounted by cupolas derived from Parigi's Garden of Calypso. Carew's *Coelum Britannicum* included a scene of ruins, the wings of which were a replica of Parigi's Palace of Fame, and Parigi's ornate design for the ship of Amerigo Vespucci was certainly the basis for the wings of Jones's Indian shore and sea in *The Temple of Love*, 1635.

The Queen and her ladies staged another pastoral, Montagu's *The Shepherd's Paradise*, at Somerset House in 1633, of which we possess drawings for the proscenium and the standing scene, another landscape of trees and hillocks with a palace and formal garden behind. Two relieve scenes are also extant, one of a domed temple with tombs, the other of an arch through which is seen a hillock with steps leading up to an ornamental pavilion. Whether there were any three-dimensional elements in them we do not know. The tree wings were retained throughout but the back shutter of the palace was drawn to reveal first one and then the other of these two further sets behind.

Once again a great mound rose from beneath the stage in *Coelum Britannicum* until it completely covered the scene and, after the masquers had made their entrance from a cave below, it sank again. 'This strange spectacle gave great cause for admiration but especially how so huge a machine, could come from under the Stage, which was but six foot high.' Professor Nicoll conjectures that it was made in sections with a masking piece for the first one. It served the purpose of concealing a change from a mountain to a garden. A huge cloud of several colours came from the side and broke open to show Eternity seated on a globe surrounded with beams of light. No wonder Sir Henry Herbert considered this the noblest of all the masques he had seen.

Sir William Davenant started his collaboration with Jones in *The Temple of Love*, 1635. It was the last masque given in the Banqueting Hall for fear that the smoke from the candles might damage Rubens's ceiling. A specially built masquing house succeeded it in 1638.

For this masque, which had an Indian setting and Persian habits, we have several designs. The Indian scene of rocks and palm trees was adapted from Parigi. A puzzling two-tiered design (Plate 3) corresponds in the upper half with the Indian scene but in the border with *Coelum Britannicum*. John Webb may have assisted Jones in *The Triumph of Peace*, 1634, but was more certainly involved in the pastoral, *Florimène*, 1635. This is well documented in a plan of the hall seating, a ground plan and section of the stage and several drawings of the scenes. Behind a forestage of some 7 feet in depth stands the proscenium arch. The four pairs of wings are still angled on the Serlian model; behind them are two grooves for two pairs of shutters which, when opened, could discover four different relieve scenes backed by a final cloth. The wings were constant throughout and represented the Isle of Delos with woods and cottages in front of a shutter depicting a landscape and distant sea (Plate 4). The first relieve scene was of a classical temple of Diana for the introduction. The pastoral itself had *intermedii* of the four seasons, for all of which we have designs. Three were relieve scenes. Winter is a snowy landscape with bare trees, a central cottage and clouds above. Spring is a formal garden with parterres, bowers and a distant villa viewed through piers and a balustrade. The summer landscape is of cornfields with a river spanned by a bridge and in the distance a building with a tower. A vintage scene in open country with a vine trellis and a distant lake and mountains represents autumn. Each of these scenes had a pair

26

PLATE 3. Inigo Jones, two-tiered scene for *Temple of Love*.

of narrow profiled wings to frame it, showing that relieve
scenes were on two planes. The last scene of all was another
temple of Diana, painted on the shutter. This was not a
spectacular piece, but it well demonstrates the variety which

PLATE 4. Inigo Jones, pastoral scene for *Florimène*.

could be achieved by the three elements of wings, shutters and scenes of relieve.

The Queen desired Jones to devise a masque that would 'give occasion for variety of Scenes, strange apparitions, Songs, Musick and dancing of severall kinds'. For this Davenant adapted a text from Cini's *Notte d'Amore* performed in Florence in 1608. Jones produced for this masque, *Luminalia*, 1638, the most romantic of his scenes. This may have been inspired by the engraving of a moonlight landscape by Elsheimer.[17] It has

17. Roy Strong citing F. Saxl and R. Wittkower, *British Art and the Mediterranean*, 1948, p. 45.

been pointed out that the grey wash technique resembles that in landscape sketches by Claude. It has a new note of dreamy stillness, deep shadows and reflections, and is described as 'all of darknesse, the neerer part woody and farther off more open with a calme River, that tooke the shadowes of the Trees by the light of the Moone that appear'd shining in the River, there being no more light to lighten the whole Scene than served to distinguish the several grounds, that seemed to run farre in from the eye'. There are drawings of the full scene with four pairs of wings and of a variant back scene splashed with paint and therefore almost certainly the one used. (Plate 5). A relieve scene of the City of Sleep on a rainbow was viewed behind 'Mountains of gold, Tower falling, Windmills, and other extravagant edifices'.

PLATE 5. Inigo Jones, night scene from *Luminalia*.

The last masque of all, Davenant's *Salmacida Spolia*, 1638, was the most advanced in technique, as is evident from the ground plan and section.[18] Jones here abandoned the angled wings for flat ones set in grooves so that for the first time they could be changed as well as the back shutters and relieves. This was not Jones's invention as it had been employed in Italy from the beginning of the century. Jones had in fact used the technique two years previously at a visit of the King and Queen to Oxford[19] which so impressed the Queen that she requested that the cloths and perspectives be sent to Hampton Court for her own players. It was the last of Jones's refinements for changeable scenery. In this masque the wings had four changes, being slid one behind another in a set of grooves. They measured 22 feet in the front, diminishing to 14 feet at the rear. Behind the back shutters were three relieve scenes and on either side of these seats for the masquers which could be let down under the stage. Above cloud borders hung in front of the shutters in upper grooves with another transverse border which joined them into one heaven. They could be changed along with the wings below. Under the stage a capstan is shown for the ascent and descent of deities.

In the two opening scenes Jones exploited a change from stormy landscape with a shutter of a wild sea to one of calm with a tranquil back scene of cornfields and villages in open country. The third change was to rocks with a desolate cloud-topped mountain behind. This was in two tiers as later the lower shutter drew to discover the King and his masquers on the Throne of Honour adorned with palm trees and statues of ancient heroes. After they had descended, a great, multi-coloured cloud came down to mid-stage and opened to reveal the Queen and her ladies wreathed in tinsel and reflected light. This machine replaced the Throne of Honour which sank under the stage. When the King and Queen had returned

18. R. Southern, 'Observations on Lansdowne Ms. No. 1171', *Theatre Notebook*, October 1947, Vol. 2.
19. Anthony à Wood, *History and Antiquities of the University of Oxford*, 1742–1746, Vol. 2, pp. 407–414, quoted by Campbell.

to the hall after the dances, a set of magnificent buildings in selected types of architecture was exhibited with a back scene of a bridge over a river on which people and coaches were depicted passing, and beyond a perspective of the suburbs of a city. A ground row in front of the bridge served to conceal the stage floor. From the upper section three clouds appeared, with eight people representing the spheres in the centre, and musicians at the sides, which covered the upper scene. Beyond came yet another revelation of a heaven with three rows of deities which filled 'all the scenes with apparitions and harmony' and concluded the splendours of Jones's final work.

The masques had evolved from static to dynamic, from an unchanging scene to scenes in constant motion with stages that rose and fell. Bacon, though regarding masques as toys, yet admitted that 'the alteration of scenes so it be quietly and without noise are things of great beauty and pleasure for they feed and relieve the eye before it be full of the same object. . . . Let the scenes abound with light, especially coloured and varied'.[20]

Motion and light are among the chief impressions one receives from the description of the scenes of the later masques. Lights shone from a myriad candles and coloured lamps and through transparencies to illuminate both scenes and brilliantly coloured, baroque costumes. The key note is Jones's word 'harmony'. Jonson's ironical quip that 'painting and carpentry were the soul of the masque' was hardly justified. It was rather the classical, ordered harmony of the Renaissance in which musical, pictorial and mobile elements were fused into the unity that the theatre perpetually strives for. The world of Jones was an ideal world as befitted the entertainment of princes. Even its storms, its desolate places and its horrid hells had no immediate reality but provided the necessary contrasts to its tranquil groves, its pastoral landscapes and its celestial glories. Its illusion was not of the everyday world and its perspective illusion was a perfect expression of it—content and form were in accord.

20. 'Of Masques and Triumphs', 1625.

31

CHAPTER III

The Caroline Stage and the Davenant Operas

Scenery in the Caroline Theatres

The first covered theatre to be used professionally in the 17th century was the second Blackfriars, which was taken over by the King's company in 1608. Of the others which followed the most important were the Phoenix (1617) and Salisbury Court (1629). They were known as private theatres, though they were public, in contradistinction to the group of open air theatres. For the first time on the public stage performances were given at night by candlelight. We have little direct evidence of their arrangements and we must assume that they had the thrust stages of the Elizabethan theatres with similar dispersed scenery. The question as to whether, or how far, they accommodated Italianate scenery is a moot one and has been the subject of argument among scholars.[21] Many of the plays presented were also given by the companies at court where we know they were provided with scenery. Whether this was ever transferred from banqueting or other halls to these theatres is difficult to assess. Such evidence as there is for the production of plays with changeable scenery is to be found in stage directions, which are not necessarily indications of what took place, and in references in prologues, which can be

21. T. J. King, 'The Staging of Plays at the Phoenix in Drury Lane, 1617–1642', *Theatre Notebook*, 1965; Kenneth Richards, G. E. Bentley.

variously interpreted. A case can be made out for some of Nabbes's plays, the most convincing being for *Microcosmus*, 'a moral masque' at Salisbury Court, 1637, which has elaborate stage directions for a special proscenium, two perspectives of ruins and clouds, scenic pieces of a sphere, rock, and throne, and a front shutter which covered scene changes, a forerunner of the 19th century carpenter's scene. But the scenery may have been wishful thinking for a court or private performance and never carried out.

There is more substantial evidence for Suckling's *Aglaura*, Blackfriars, 1638. Suckling was a wealthy courtier and, according to Aubrey who is not altogether reliable, he provided suits of gold and silver, and his play had also 'some scaenes to it, which in those days were only used at masques'. Aubrey is, however, backed up by a rival dramatist, Brome, who poured scorn on its 'gaudy Sceane', and by an apparent reference in the prologue to Newcastle's *The Country Captain* at Blackfriars:

> he does not meane
> To show you here a glorious painted Scene,
> With various doores, to stand instead of wit.

An interesting suggestion has been made that when the tragicomic version of the play was given at Jones's Cockpit-in-Court his scenes for *Luminalia* may have been used, as both had night scenes, but whether the elaborate Masquing House scenery could have been fitted into the arch of the Cockpit seems dubious.[22]

There is one further piece of evidence that the players were capable of handling perspective scenery in their theatre. When the Queen borrowed Jones's scenes from Oxford, the University made a condition that they were not to come into the hands of professional companies.

One instance of scenery being used in a private house was for Fane's *Candy Restored*, which was acted by his children at

22. John Freehafer, 'The Italian Night Piece and Suckling's *Aglaura*', *Journal of English and Germanic Philology*, 1968.

his seat at Apthorpe in 1640. A ground plan and section[23] show that there were three wings slanted towards the back of the stage and a traverse, and that they were changed by the *scena versatilis* method, swivelled by ropes attached to the bottom of each wing. It is surprising to find the advanced technique of wing and back change at a private performance and it is indicative of the influence of court scenery.

There was one attempt to build a theatre which could accommodate Italianate scenes. Davenant, who had collaborated with Jones in later masques, obtained a patent in 1639 to erect a playhouse in Fleet Street. Though the scheme came to nothing it was evidence of the way the wind was blowing. Davenant may have been aware of Torelli's Teatro di San Cassiano in Venice, built in 1637 to house Italian operas with elaborate scenic effects, and may have wished to establish an English counterpart.

John Webb and the Davenant Operas

The civil war and then the interregnum closed all theatres for nearly twenty years. Puritan domination ensured an almost complete arrest of further developments just when the scenery of the English court stage had at last drawn level with that of the Continent. In Italy in the meantime opera was the ruling passion and this necessitated sophisticated scenery with many changes. John Evelyn, who visited Venice in 1645, records thirteen in *Ercole in Lidia* and Robert Bargrave, who followed him in 1655, notes 'Scenes set out in rare paintings and all magnificent costumes; intermixing most incomparable apparitions and motions in the aire and on the Seas, governed so by Machines'.[24]

In spite of the clamp down on entertainments a few got through. The first was Shirley's masque, *Cupid and Death,*

23. Henry E. Huntington Library. Reproduced, Nicoll, *Stuart Masques.*
24. Quoted by E. Walter White, 'English Travellers at Italian Opera Performances in the XVIIth Century', *Theatre Research,* 1970.

presented in 1653 before the Portuguese Ambassador. Shirley tells us that the 'Scenes wanted no elegance, or curiosity for the delight of the spectator' but does not say who designed them. According to the stage directions they consisted of a forest with a tavern on a hillside which changed to a garden with walks, arbours and a fountain, one of the arbours being practicable. The second change was to the Elysian fields where the masquers appeared in glorious habits and decorated seats. A machine brought Mercury down from a cloud.

When Davenant returned to London in 1656 he started to pursue his ambition to introduce perspective scenery onto the public stage. After a preliminary Entertainment at Rutland House, in which the merits and demerits of scenery were debated, he organised there 'a Representation by the Art of Prospective in Scenes, And the Story sung in Recitative Musick'. Though Davenant protected himself by stressing perspective as the main feature, *The Siege of Rhodes* was an early type of opera. This is the first occasion on which we can be certain that perspective scenery was used on a public stage in this country and fortunately we possess a plan, section and designs for it.[25] Davenant obtained the services of John Webb, Jones's assistant in the last masques, for the scenery. Webb was faced with a problem because the stage only measured 22 feet 4 inches wide and 18 feet deep. The back shutters were only 9 feet wide and 7 feet 6 inches high, which Davenant laments was too 'narrow an allowance for the fleet of Solyman the Magnificent, his army, the Island of Rhodes, and the varieties attending the siege of the city.' There was no space either for wing changes or machinery and the forestage was limited to 6 inches; but Webb managed five scene changes, including two relieves—a considerable achievement. The proscenium was formed of rusticated columns and emblematical military decorations. There were three pairs of standing profiled rock wings. The first shutter (Plate 6) was a view of Rhodes based on two topographical prints and reasonably correct,

25. B. M. Lansdowne Ms. 1171; designs at Chatsworth.

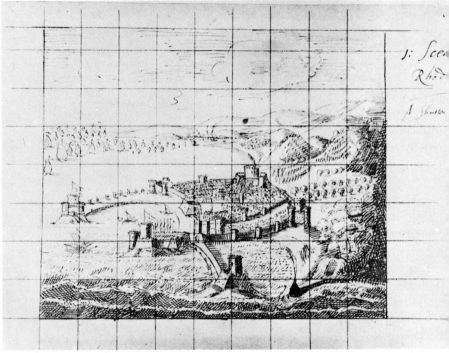

PLATE 6. John Webb, *Siege of Rhodes*. A shutter of Rhodes.

even to the windmills on the mole, which are still there. The second shutter was of the besieged city, showing the Turkish camp before the walls and the blockading fleet. This drew to discover the first relieve scene of Solyman's canopied throne with two flanking columns on front wings and with rows of tents painted on a backcloth. The floor was divided into receding squares on the Serlian model. The shutter of the besieged city closed over this to conceal the change to the second relieve of Mount Philermus with Solyman's army and a bastion on opposite sides of the stage. The final shutter was of the assault on the city with the English bulwark prominent and the army painted on the canvas, a long lasting convention which Jones had used and may have inherited from French precedents. In spite of ten changes the scenes did not coincide with the acts, nor did they always represent the background to the action. The same back shutter served for Turks and Rhodians and no provision was made for Ianthe's tent in Sicily. The audience was no doubt content with the variety of scenes and regarded them as suggestive backgrounds to the action rather than illustrations of it. Webb established a pattern of proscenium, wings, back shutters in grooves and relieve scenes behind, which he transported from the masques and which became the staple stage convention well into the 19th century.

Davenant's next shows were *The Cruelty of the Spaniards in Peru* at the Cockpit in Drury Lane in 1659, and *Sir Francis Drake* in the same year. Both had perspective scenes but we do not know whether Webb was responsible for them. Again only the shutters changed and again some attempt was made at local colour, a landscape of the West Indies in the first and in the second a wood of pines and coconut palms, with monkeys, apes and parrots painted on their boughs. Evelyn hardly surprisingly remarked that the scenes were after the Italian manner but inferior in magnificence.[26]

Webb, who bridged the gap between the Jacobean masques and the Restoration scenic stage, was responsible for one more play at court. In 1665 Boyle's heroic tragedy, *Mustapha*, was staged in the Hall Theatre in Whitehall which Webb had converted into a permanent court theatre with a grid for hanging frames. Carpenters made models of the scenes and frames and Robert Streeter painted the scenery. The proscenium was of Tuscan columns surmounted by a broken pediment and was provided with balconies, but not with proscenium doors. Four scenes, for which we have designs, were remarkably similar to those for *The Siege of Rhodes*. For instance, Solyman's pavilion (Plate 7), like his throne, was a practicable central piece, though in this case in a draped alcove, and Buda Beleagured had a family resemblance to Rhodes in like plight. The tents and painted armies also recall those of the assault on Rhodes. There was an additional pair

26. *Diary*, May 5, 1659.

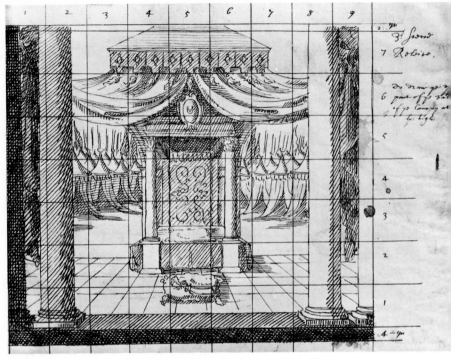

PLATE 7. John Webb, *Mustapha*. Solyman's pavilion.

of wings, but the same number of relieve scenes. Permanent clouds appear to have been fastened to the grid. A fifth scene associated with this play represents a forecourt of columns with a back scene of house and gardens. The first wings appear to be the same as those of Solyman's pavilion, but the drawing is in a nobler, severer style.

By the nature of the circumstances Webb's scenery cannot compete in splendour with that of Jones; in comparison it is more pedestrian and lacking in imaginative quality. The ideal world of the masques had vanished and been replaced by the heroic one of clashing armies, camps and sieges. Because the dramas of Davenant and Boyle were set in definite places far from the never-never land of the court masques, Webb was required to attempt some degree of topographical reproduction and so took one step forward towards realism.

38

CHAPTER IV

The Restoration

Early Scenery

Charles II had spent some of his exile in Paris and had probably seen the work of Torelli, who had built a stage in the Italian manner for Louis XIV with scenery and machinery. Torelli introduced simultaneous wing changes by a counterweight method in Venice. In Paris he made a spectacular success with the opera, *La Finta Pazza*, 1645, and the designs for this were engraved. So were those of Corneille's *Andromède*, 1650, another splendid production. The King no doubt wished to see something of the kind on his restoration to the throne and in 1661 a troupe of French comedians under Channouveau was temporarily installed at the Cockpit in Drury Lane (the erstwhile Phoenix).

Among their offerings was *The Descent of Orpheus into Hell*, for which the English translation describes the 'Great Machines'. The scenes were many, including rocks and a grotto from which a dragon issued, whilst above a heaven opened to discover Juno in her chariot drawn up and down by eagles; a Doric palace which changed to a garden with a globe in which was the palace of the sun; the banks of Acheron with Charon's barque; a dismal hell with Pluto's palace; and a cypress grove in which Orpheus appeared under an arch of trees and flowers. These scenes are the familiar ones of the baroque stage. Pepys, however, saw the company and found the scenes 'nasty and out of order and poor', so obviously they did not live up to the description and probably could not be staged in full at the Cockpit.

More important were the patents granted to the courtiers

Davenant and Killigrew authorising them to set up two theatres with scenes and to charge for admission. Killigrew's patent specifically stated that these charges should take account of his great expenses on scenes and new decorations such as 'have not been formerly used'. Thus the step was taken to introduce Italian scenery into the public theatre as a regular accompaniment to all types of play. Plays at court had hitherto been confined to pastorals; now the range of scenes had to be wider and more realistic to fit dramas and comedies. Palaces and temples were still needed but they were supplemented by rooms, taverns and coffee houses and the milieux of ordinary life. Since the companies worked on a repertory system of daily change of play, they had to build up stock scenery which could serve for several productions. The managers, with their limited resources, could only occasionally supply new scenes and found it less costly to indulge in new costumes.

Visual documentation for the period is poor; a mere handful of designs exists, apart from Webb's *Mustapha* at court. We have to rely on authors' stage directions, which may not always have been implemented, descriptions by foreign visitors, and comments by Pepys and Evelyn.

Both Davenant and Killigrew followed French precedents by adapting tennis courts for their theatres, but, whereas Killigrew's in Vere Street could not accommodate scenery and was only temporary, Davenant's at Lincoln's-Inn-Fields introduced scenery from the start. He opened with a revival of his *Siege of Rhodes*, 1661, to which he added a second part with two new settings—one of Roxalana's rich pavilion and the other of Rhodes by night with the palace on fire. Dr. Southern points out that rock wings would have been inconsistent with the former and suggests that they were changed. In the prologue to Part 2 Davenant apologised for his 'contracted scenes' which in his narrow theatre could not compare in extent or depth of perspective with those which some spectators had seen in Italy or Paris. He promised that, if money

40

could be obtained, his scenes should be wider 'And move by greater Engines'. All the same, Pepys, an average playgoer, was impressed: 'the scene opened; which indeed is very fine and magnificent'. Pepys was also present when *Hamlet* was 'done with Scenes very well', the first Shakespearean performance on a picture stage.[27]

The scenery consisted of wings and back shutters but there was one vital difference from the former arrangements. The shutters were no longer bunched together as hitherto but the grooves in which they worked were separated. This meant that a group of actors and stage furniture could be discovered by the drawing of a shutter and, conversely, could be closed upon, leaving other players to continue the action against a fresh background. This was a new conception of the function of scenery, to serve a dramatic purpose as well as a decorative one. The theatres inherited from the Elizabethans large forestages, to which were added permanent proscenium arches which masked the scenery behind and contained two or three doors of entrance on each side surmounted by windows. A good deal of the action took place on the forestage, but some was played within the scenes. The forestages were a specifically English feature which brought the actors well out amidst the audience of the boxes and galleries. Unlike the Continental theatres, there was a clear division of the two parts of the stage by the proscenium arch. The perspective scenery was more of a background than it was abroad, where the actors played entirely within, cut off from the auditorium by the proscenium arch.

Many early plays must have had new scenes until a stock was created. Thus Tuke's *Adventures of Five Hours* had three houses, a garden and a view of Seville. A practicable centre door was cut in the back shutter, providing an additional entrance.

Killigrew moved into his new Theatre Royal in Bridges Street, Drury Lane, on May 7, 1663, when *The Humorous*

27. *Diary*, July 2, August 24, 1661.

Lieutenant was performed with scenes. Pepys saw *The Faithful Shepherdess* on June 13 and records that the house was thronged 'for the Scenes sake, which is very fine indeed'. Killigrew had a scheme to set up a 'nursery', or actors' training centre, for the performance of plays and operas with the best scenes and machines for which he intended to import Italian painters.[28] Though it came to nothing it is evidence of the desire to imitate Italian operatic spectacle. French and Italian troupes, who generally brought their own scenery with them, were frequent visitors at court from 1663 onwards.[29]

So far there had not been much opportunity for magnificence or machines. Stock scenes of chambers, streets, woods, gardens, prisons and palaces were accumulating. Several well known London localities, such as Covent Garden, Whitehall, the Mall and the New Exchange, were exhibited in comedies, providing illustrations of the recognisable world in which the spectators moved. With the advent of Dryden's tragedies a new heroic, exotic note was sounded, in succession to the magic symbolism of the masques. *The Indian Queen*, Theatre Royal, 1664, marks a new departure into splendour. Evelyn praised its beautiful 'rich scenes as the like had never been seene here or haply (except rarely) elsewhere in a mercenary theatre'.[30] Among the scenes was a golden Temple of the Sun with a blood-stained altar. The scenery and habits were used the following year for the sequel, *The Indian Emperor*. Machines were employed in Dryden's *Rival Ladies*, Theatre Royal, 1664, in swift motion for descents and in slow for the arising of a flaming black chariot from below.

Isaac Fuller, a well known decorative and scene painter, was engaged on a scene of Elysium for *Tyrannic Love*, 1669, for the large sum of £335. It occupied him six weeks but the managers refused to pay him more than £40 on the grounds that he had contracted to finish it in a fortnight in as good a

28. *Ibid.*, August 2, 1664.
29. S. Rosenfeld, *Foreign Theatrical Companies in Great Britain in the 17th and 18th Centuries*, Society for Theatre Research, 1955.
30. *Diary*, August 12, 1664.

fashion as scenes by the other artists for the Theatre and that he had lost them custom and reputation because he had painted but meanly. Fuller brought a suit against the theatre and won it, being supported by the court painter, Streeter, who gave evidence that he was the quickest of artists and that six weeks was a fair time.[31] The case gives evidence of the care lavished on one particular scene.

Two other scenes of this time are mentioned by Pepys: 'a fine scene of the Senate' for *Cataline* and 'a good scene of a town on fire' for *The Island Princess*.[32] Boyle's *Guzman*, Lincoln's-Inn-Fields, 1669, is a typical example of a mixture of old and new scenes. Two of the former had been used in previous plays by the author, a garden scene from his *Tryphon* and the Queen of Hungary's chamber from *Mustapha*, as well as a chimney and a chamber flat scene. New were a 'Black Scene' for an astrologer's cabinet and a 'Flat Scene' of a Piazza and grove of trees.

How good was the scenery in this first decade? Flecknoe in his *Discourse of the English Stage*, 1664, considered that we could not approach Italian or French models or compare in magnificence with the scenery of former masques and plays: 'Italians this latter age are the greatest Masters, the *French* good proficients, and we in England only Schollars and Learners yet, having proceeded no further than to bare painting, and not arriv'd to the stupendious wonders of your great Ingeniers, especially not knowing yet how to place our Lights, for the more advantage and illuminating of the Scenes'. It was machinery and lighting in which we were deficient. As for painting, Flecknoe considered that our scenes 'for cost and ornament, are arriv'd at the heighth of Magnificence'. This is borne out by the verdict of foreign witnesses. In 1663 Sorbière commented on the number of scene changes and perspectives and another Frenchman, Monconys, found the scene changes as well as the machines ingenious. Much the same view was

31. L. Hotson, *Commonwealth and Restoration Stage*, 1928, p. 250.
32. *Diary*, December 19, 1668; January 7, 1669.

expressed by Chappuzeau in 1667, who praised our theatres for decorations and changes and gave it as his opinion that the machinery at Lincoln's-Inn-Fields was on a par with that of the Italians'. Finally, Cosimo III remarked that the scenery was 'very light, capable of a great many changes, and embellished with beautiful landscapes'.[33] Evidently English theatres were outstanding in their manipulation of scene changes and this may have been due to the groove system as against that of the Continental understage wagons.

New Theatres, New Spectacles

Davenant died in 1668 but his company brought to completion the sumptuous Dorset Garden Theatre, which they opened in 1671, and on June 26 Evelyn saw 'the new Machines for the intended Scenes which were indeed very costly'. It is possible that Betterton had recently visited France and may have taken ideas from Vigarani's famous Salle des Machines in Paris which was an outstanding influence on scenic display. Dorset Garden became the home of spectacle; Brunet considered it incomparably more beautiful than the French theatres[34] and the engravings depict an ornate proscenium with a music room above (Plate 8). The operatic *Macbeth* of 1673 was the first of a long series of dramatic operas given at the theatre in which the machines, including those for its famous flying hordes of witches, were invented and worked by Henry Wright. Machines became the rage:

> We then to flying Witches did advance
> And for your pleasure traffic'd into France . . .
> We have machines to some perfection brought.
> (Shadwell, epilogue, *The Tempest*, 1674)

33. S. Sorbière, *Relation d'un Voyage en Angleterre*, 1664, translated into English, 1709; S. Chappuzeau, *L'Europe Vivante*, 1667, pp. 214–215; *Travels of Cosmo III*, pp. 190–191, quoted Hotson, pp. 234–235.
34. Cited by Hotson, pp. 234–235.

Other dramatists were not at all pleased as they felt the audience was being distracted from their plays by its craving for novelty:

> Devils and witches must each Scene inspire
> Wit rowls in Waves, and showers down in fire.
> (Rawlings, prologue to *Tunbridge Wells*, 1678)

Dryden did not fail to discredit the taste for machines, 'those wick'd Engines', though his own 'operas' provided opportunity for their use. In the prologue to *Albion and Albanius*, one of the most spectacular creations, he gibed:

> The Wise Italians first invented show;
> Thence into France the Noble Pageant past;
> 'Tis England's Credit to be cozn'd last.

The text of Settle's *Empress of Morocco* supplies us with five engravings which give an idea of the scenery. The vaulted dungeon (Plate 8) is the most enclosed setting for which we have an illustration. The customary squared floor and the lighting by a single lamp are noteworthy. The second engraving is 'The Prospect of a large River with a glorious Fleet of Ships' painted on the back shutter which opened to discover a dance of Moors who brought on a prop in the form of a palm tree. The fourth engraving (Plate 9) is of interest as showing a masque scene of a flaming hell with devils rising in traps and flying in the air. Though crude, it is an obvious descendant from Inigo Jones. The last engraving shows tortures painted on a backcloth, a scene of horror which Jones would never have created. The illustrations are remarkable for their variety of style: medieval in the dungeon, exotic in the dance and classical in the harbour. The scene shifts did not accord with the acts but with the frequent changes of locality; thus a palace scene opened after only three lines to discover a bedchamber.

The operatic *Tempest*, 1674, had twelve changes with five different scenes. The curtain rose to display a new frontispiece

PLATE 8. Settle's *Empress of Morocco*. Prison scene.

PLATE 9. *Empress of Morocco*, Masque scene of hell.

or false proscenium of Corinthian columns wreathed with flying cupids and two figures of our old friend Fame perched on the cornice. Angels were placing the King's arms in the centre of the pediment. This framed a scene of a rocky coast and tempestuous sea in continuous agitation and the now familiar spirits were rising, flying and crossing one another. As the ship sank the whole house was darkened and a shower of fire fell. This ability to darken the house was new. The chandelier must have risen above, the footlights been lowered and shields dropped over the wing lights. Illumination returned as the scene changed to the traditional three-perspective cypress walls leading to Prospero's cave. The middle prospect was of great depth, so presumably used the back scenic area. Throughout four acts this scene alternated with one of the wilder part of the island with a prospect of the distant sea, painted no doubt on a shutter. In the last act this shutter was replaced by a rock one with a rocky arch and calm sea. The wings must here at least have been changed from cypresses to rocks. The final scene was of a rising sun with myriads of aerial spirits painted on the cloth. These changes could easily have been accommodated on a stage which Dr. Southern has calculated was equipped with shutters at four depths, each with two grooves, which would allow of eight different scenes.

A month before *The Tempest* was produced at Dorset Garden, Killigrew opened his new theatre in Drury Lane. It was almost certainly by Christopher Wren[35] and, like its rival, was an amphitheatre in shape, though neither so large nor so splendid. The curved forestage projected 20 feet into the auditorium. The proscenium arch was furnished with two stage doors on each side divided by Corinthian pilasters of

35. A section drawing among Wren's papers at All Soul's, Oxford, was identified as the theatre by Hamilton Bell, 'Contributions to the History of the English Playhouse', *Architectural Record*, 1913, Vol. 33, pp. 359–368. See also, *The Theatre Royal, Drury Lane, and the Royal Opera House, Covent Garden*, Survey of London, ed. F. H. W. Sheppard, 1970, Vol. 34, pp. 42–45.

diminishing height and width as they ascended to the scenic
area. This perspective handling linked the design of the stage
to that of the auditorium, an admirable feature continued in
the 18th century. The stage was 20 feet deep and took four
sets of wings, but only three sets of shutters, one less than at
Dorset Garden. The back stage was even longer, at 25 feet,
and accommodated further scenery as well as a scene dock.
The scenes for this back stage were often known as long
scenes, such as 'long wood' and 'long street', and were the
successors of the relieve scenes. Drury Lane was intended as
much for plays as for spectacles; hence its comparative simplicity. The engraving of the French opera, *Ariane* (Plate 10),

PLATE 10. Perrin's *Ariane*.

given on the second night, is certainly more restrained and classical than those for *The Empress of Morocco*, even though chariots descended and ascended with gods. The forestage is foreshortened in the engraving and the palace sides are made to appear laterally joined, whereas they were certainly painted on wings in perspective. The scallop shell was practicable and bore three nymphs.

The court theatre now took a secondary place as both Charles II and James II were patrons of the public theatres, and the Hall Theatre could not compete with the two new ones. However, by examining the accounts, Eleanore Boswell discovered illuminating information about the productions there. New scenery was prepared for the Queen's masque, 1671, consisting of a pair of shutters and four pairs of wings of boscage [woods] for which Streeter was paid £5 and £20 respectively. There was a garden scene, a mill scene and a practicable door. The painting of clouds cost £4·16 but, as in Jones's time, sky-coloured calico served as a false ceiling in the theatre. Streeter painted a great back cloth of rusticated stonework measuring 50 yards and an arch and cross piece of stonework of $17\frac{1}{2}$ yards. This was subsequently painted over to represent sea and sky. Streeter also painted long pieces of sky which were nailed to a fixed border. The carpenter's work included making a pair of shutters, two relieves, cutting a trap door and making a 5 foot square platform in the clouds.

Streeter, who was Serjeant Painter to the King, was responsible for Crowne's masque, *Calisto*, 1675, with *intermezzi*, which was the most spectacular of the court shows. Evelyn thought him an 'excellent painter of perspective and land-scape' and admired as 'very glorious' his scenery for Dryden's *Conquest of Granada* at court in 1671.[36] *Calisto* was performed chiefly by the royal children with professional dancers and singers. Though the stage was extended a yard further into the pit, the proscenium was also advanced, forming a picture stage. New red, white and blue curtains were drawn to

50   36. *Diary*, January 20, 1675; February 9, 1671.

discover a prospect of Somerset House and the Thames with clouds above painted on a pair of shutters 15 feet wide and 14 feet 9 inches high with two wings of 4 feet wide by 14 feet 9 inches high. On the upper stage the cloud shutters were 15 feet by 14 feet with two wings. The shutters drew to display a transparency of a Temple of Fame on frames covered with varnished silk lit from behind. A scene of boscage on another shutter and wings followed, and the side walls of the theatre between the wings were also painted in boscage, presumably for the benefit of those who sat at the side and could see through the gaps between them. For the finale the shutter drew to reveal the 'glory' or group of deities above. For this Richard Ryder, the master carpenter, constructed a back piece with a circle, 11 feet 6 inches by 7 feet 6 inches, cut in it. A transparency provided the requisite aura of light, and additional lights shone down from steps behind. Some idea of the appearance of such a glory may be gleaned from Streeter's ceiling fresco in the Sheldonian at Oxford, where it is surrounded by small clouds. All in all, Streeter painted 139 yards of cloud work. Upper clouds were circular and were fastened behind the shutters. Profiled scenery was in use not only for the clouds but for an arbour and flowery bank. £107 was spent on wax candles and torches alone, and 96 tin sconces with reflector plates were nailed to the back of the clouds. Footlights were installed in a trough. These accounts provide us with the only details we have of scene construction in the period.

Calisto followed masque precedent in being based on Greek fable. The great series of dramatic operas at Dorset Garden also drew themes from this source, as well as from British legends, and so owed much to the masques in subject as well as in staging.

Shadwell, in his preface to *Psyche*, 1675, admits his indebtedness to the French opera presented at the Théâtre des Machines in 1671: 'For several things concerning the Decoration of the Play, I am oblig'd to the *French*, and for the Design of Two of the onely moving Scenes in the *French*, which I may say without vanity are very much improv'd, being wrought up with more Art'. The scenery was painted by Thomas Stephenson and cost over £800. Stephenson, a landscape and architectural artist, was a pupil of Robert Aggas, a scene painter who worked at Drury Lane.[37] Shadwell claimed in his prologue that 'His bus'ness now is to show splendid Scenes, T'interpret 'twixt the Audience and Machines'.

There were in fact plenty of the latter, though the eight settings of baroque type were the main attraction. A deep walk in a wood was succeeded by a Temple of Apollo surmounted by a cupola with Doric columns ornamented with gold. This gave way to a rocky desert with caves, cliffs and precipices, which parallels the first *intermède* of the French *Psyché*, and Shadwell then takes from the second *intermède* his Palace of Cupid decorated with Corinthian columns wreathed with roses and cupids. This made use of the whole stage as two courts were divided by three arches. It was followed by a city street with a triumphal arch, through which a piazza and obelisk were seen, probably a painted front scene. The traditional stately garden, also taken from *Psyché*, was presumably a long scene, since a further vista of cypress walk was shown through an arbour. The golden statues which lined the walks descended to dance and cupids flew from their pedestals to strew the stage with flowers. After this pretty scene had vanished, Psyche was discovered by contrast in a desert again, as in the French version. Hell with its burning ruins, its devils and its damned followed. Pluto on his throne with Proserpine at his feet rose from under the stage and through the throne's fiery pillars were seen the gates of hell and a flaming lake, as in the fourth *intermède* of *Psyché*. A scene covered in for the final change to the heavens, in the highest part of which was the Palace of Jupiter ornamented in gold, whilst below was

---

37. Horace Walpole, *Anecdotes of Painting in England*, Vol. 1, p. 304. Aggas and Samuel Towers petitioned for £40 in 1677 and £32 in 1682 for work carried out at Drury Lane.

another cut temple, through which the sun's beams broke. Several semi-circular clouds which took up the breadth of the house descended with Apollo and musicians and, lastly, Jupiter, accompanied by Cupid and Psyche, descended in a machine.

This fine spectacle for the first time rivalled those of the court masques. Any one of its scenes might have been devised by Jones—the iconography had not changed with the transition to the public stage. It was eight years before such another spectacle was seen.

Albion and Albanius, 1685, like Jonson's masques, was devised as a flattering tribute to the King. Dryden informs us that the elaborate stage directions stemmed from Betterton, and this lends them authenticity. The scenery, like the text, was a mixed bag of the baroque and the localised. It included an ornate new frontispiece with symbolic and decorative adornments. The opening street of palaces led to the Royal Exchange and was flanked by copies of statues of Charles I and Charles II. A further perspective of arch and street was shown through the open arch of the Exchange. The clouds of the upper stage divided and Juno appeared in a machine drawn by peacocks. As it moved forward in its descent the tail of the peacock opened and almost filled the stage by means of a fan machine that derived from the Florentine fête of 1586. Iris also appeared in a large cloud machine and, after the deities had re-ascended, part of the scene was removed to display four of the triumphal arches erected for Charles II's coronation. A total change then took place to a 'poetical hell' with an arch of fire and three pyramids of flames in perpetual agitation. This was followed by another topographical scene taken from mid-Thames including York Stairs to Whitehall and Millbank on one side and the Saw Mill to the Bishop's Palace on the other. The further part of the heavens opened discovering a machine; as this moved forward the clouds in front of it divided, revealing Apollo and, as they fell lower, his horses appeared in a ray whilst a glory surrounded the

53

god. As he went from sight, Neptune and attendants arose from the water. This series of revelations by movement was typical of the baroque stage. We revert to topography with a prospect of Dover from the sea with cliff wings and a view of the pier, town and castle. The cave of Proteus, consisting of arches of rock work adorned with shells and coral, rose from the sea. Proteus sank and underwent transformations to a lion, crocodile and dragon. When the machine rose again it opened to discover Venus and Albanius in a scallop shell drawn by dolphins; this moved forward and, after its occupants were disposed on the stage, closed and sank. Another large machine descended with Apollo on a golden throne, clouds shining with gold and angels and cherubim in flight. Albion mounted the machine and was borne slowly upwards. The last scene was a walk with views of Windsor on four back scenes showing various parts of the town and castle. On the stage above was a vision of the Honours of the Garter, knights in procession and the King under a canopy with the upper end of St. George's Hall beyond. Lastly, Fame rose from mid-stage standing on a globe. The opera is remarkable not only for its multiplicity of effects but for its interspersed scenes of actual places and buildings in which it points the way towards realism.

In Betterton's adaptation of Beaumont and Fletcher's *Prophetess* to a dramatic opera in 1690 there were two notable innovations. The first was the use of a curtain which represented the interior of a palace with an arch and painted draperies. This was not to conceal a change but was a scene in itself. This 'Great Curtain' has therefore a claim to be the first drop scene. The second innovation was a machine in the final masque which was 'so large, it fills all the Space from the Frontispiece of the Stage to the farther end of the House and fixes itself by two Ladders of Clouds to the Floor'. It was divided into four separate stages depicting four palaces terminated by a glowing cloud in which was a golden chair of state. The sun broke through a cloud to create the glory.

Arthur descended by the cloud ladders, whilst from under the stage arose a garden prospect with fountains, orange trees and a middle walk leading to a palace. There were dancers on every stage in the machine. The whole upper stage in four sections came part way down, whilst by a double movement another stage ascended from below.

The Dryden-Purcell *King Arthur*, 1691, had a fresh dramatic device of ushering in scene changes by the striking or waving of a wand. Cupid thus gave the signal for the opening of a winter landscape shutter to reveal a prospect of ice and snow to the end of the stage.

The Preface to the Dryden-Purcell *Fairy Queen*, 1692, made a plea for the establishment of opera in England on the French model. Among the elaborate new scenes was one of trees arched at the side of a river. Two dragons formed another arched bridge over the river, under which two swans advanced and by a trick changed into furies. When the bridge vanished the trees reverted to their upright position. Sunrise appeared over a garden with fountains. When the vapours dissipated rows of marble columns supporting walks were revealed with stairs rising to the top of the house, probably a re-use of *The Prophetess* machinery. Juno and her peacocks again covered a scene change. Most novel was an early scene of *chinoiserie*, a transparent Chinese garden in which pedestals of China work supported porcelain vases filled with China orange trees. Everything from the architecture to the birds and beasts was in oriental style.

Settle, who was himself a machinist, devised several new effects for his *World in the Moon*, 1697. The sets were said to be different from those used in any other theatre and twice as high,[38] but the latter claim is untrue as they were nearly 30 feet high, only 2 feet higher than those for *Calisto*. Travellers reported that they excelled any seen in foreign theatres. Settle in his Epistle Dedicatory claims that 'never was such a Pile

38. Nicoll, *History of English Drama*, Vol. 1, p. 81, citing *Post Boy*, June 12–15, 1697.

of Painting rais'd upon so generous a foundation'. He had removed 'a long Heap of Rubbish, and thrown away our old *French* lumber, our Clouds of Clouts, and set the Theatrical Paintings at a much fairer Light'. This confirms that scenery had been brought from France or copied from French models after Betterton's visit in 1683.

The opera opened with the drawing of a flat scene to discover three arches of clouds extending to the roof and terminating with a further prospect of cloud work filled with figures of fame and cupids. A circular part of the back clouds rolled away to discover the moon, which was 14 feet in diameter. The moon, waning by degrees, revealed a world within of four more circles of clouds. Twelve golden chariots with twelve children representing the signs of the zodiac rode in the clouds. The third arch was withdrawn, leaving the prospect terminating in a landscape of woods, waters and a town. In the second act a palace of Cynthia, nearly 20 feet high, was supported on twelve pillars of lapis lazuli with gold and silver ornaments. Another full scene in Act III was of a palace with seven arches and pillars of white twisted marble. Its roof was enriched with panels, mouldings and carved flowers of gold, and the vista continued with Doric pillars of Egyptian marble terminating in a triumphal arch. The next change was to a full scene of a wood in which not only the back but the side scenes were cut out. The paintings are described as meeting in a circle, the first time such a phrase has been used. Was this the kind of circular perspective for which Andrea Pozzo provided plans and descriptions three years later?[39] Did Settle here anticipate Juvarra who, early in the 18th century, designed a garden pavilion in circular shape?[40] The next spectacular scene was an arbourage of nine arches, the largest number yet seen, festooned with flowers and golden ribbons. This was retained for the last scene of Cynthia's

39. *Prospettiva dei Pittori e Architetti*, Part 2, Rome, 1700; translation, 1707.
40. Victoria and Albert, reproduced Wynne Jeudwine, *Stage Designs*, 1968, Plate 7. Plates 10–12 show another circular plan by Righini, 1728.

bower, which had a prospect of terrace walks mounted one above the other on eight stages. In the centre was a flight of marble steps 24 feet high, down which figures descended from the terraces above. This set of scenes with its arbourage work stretched back 50 feet, the full extent of the house.

Settle's last great spectacle, *The Virgin Prophetess*, was given at Drury Lane in 1701. It was announced that 'for Grandeur, Decorations, Movements of Scenes' it would be infinitely superior to *The Prophetess*, which had been revived at Drury Lane the previous year, and would probably 'equal the greatest Performance of that Kind in any of the foreign Theatres'.[41] Robert Robinson painted the scenery and was paid £130, very much less than Fuller had contracted for for one scene. He was given seven weeks in which to complete the work. Robinson was a decorative artist and his painted panels in Sir John Cass's College and at the Victoria and Albert Museum show that his style was light foreshadowing the rococo, and that he was an early painter of *chinoiserie*.[42] This leads one to conjecture that he may also have painted the Chinese scenes in *King Arthur*.

The most famous scene in *The Virgin Prophetess* was a dome with semi-circularly spaced pyramids within mounted on pedestals, altogether 27 feet 6 inches high. Jones's device of a curtain to mask the lower and upper portions of the stage was developed in more elaborate fashion. The lower painted curtain hung 13 feet high and wide under the second arch; above was a prospect of the roof 11 feet high. Two life-size cupids took hold of the upper corners of the curtain and drew it up, whilst two others at the lower corners rose with it. When raised it discovered a small set of scenes 12 feet high and wide which consisted of a flat scene with three pairs of wings representing Cupid's palace with an inner prospect of a garden terminating in bowers and fountains. This formed the

41. *London Stage*, Vol. 1, p. 529, quoting *Post Boy*, May 14–16, 1700.
42. E. Croft-Murray, 'An English Painter of Chinoiseries', *Country Life Annual*, 1955.

central perspective and out of it on each side were drawn forth two further sets 12 feet 6 inches high, in unison with the middle one, the whole forming three perspectives. The painted curtain which, as it rose, masked the upper stage was then drawn higher to reveal a fourth set of scenes over the middle lower one and from this in turn issued two more scenes, one from each side, paralleling those below. This machine then filled the whole house, reaching 24 feet high. The progressive revelation of six scenes, three below followed by three above, must have been most striking.

In Act IV alone there were four changes. Again we find 'a circular piece of Painting in the manner of a large Portico' extending to the roof, through which was seen a prospect of Troy. This was snatched away to be replaced by a garden which, at a wave of Cassandra's wand, in turn vanished, revealing a view of heaven with its hierarchy of gods, to be succeeded later by a transparent hell. These four successive back stage scenes were apparently viewed through the standing pillars of the portico. Almost every known contrivance was utilised in this piece to provide constant change and movement. It is almost a compendium of devices in use on the English stage. We shall find no spectacles more elaborate in the 18th century.

Drury Lane was able to compete in spectacle with Dorset Garden in spite of its forestage having been docked 4 feet in 1696 in order to accommodate more spectators. The first proscenium doors were replaced by stage boxes and a new pair installed on the stage, which necessitated the abolition of one pair of side wings. Scenery as well as players were removed further back from the audience. Colley Cibber preferred the old stage where 'all objects were . . . drawn nearer to the senses; every painted scene was stronger; every grand scene and dance more extended'.[43] This was the beginning of the erosion of forestages which continued until they disappeared in the late 19th century.

43. *An Apology for His Life*, Everyman ed., p. 213.

The public theatre had exceeded in mechanics and mobility, though probably not in lighting, that of the court in Jones's time. How the scenery compared as art we cannot judge, since we have no visual evidence. The baroque style held the stage in this series of spectacles. The iconography did not differ much from that of Jones, but the scene designer no longer had to provide for the discovery of two sets of masquers. There were a few innovations, such as cut wings, arched trees and circular perspectives, but the chief advance was due to the fact that the new theatres had been equipped with larger and more technically sophisticated machines. They were capable of many more scene changes, ever deeper perspectives, and a multiplicity of stages at different levels. The love of show grew with what it fed on and audiences expected more and more lavish and extravagant effects. For this they were frequently admonished; and in a series of burlesques Duffett attempted the weapon of ridicule: all to no effect. The theatres were forced to supply what their patrons demanded, even to the verge of ruination.

CHAPTER V

Some
Georgian Scenes
and Scene Painters

Scene Painters

Account books of the theatres preserved from the 18th century
supply details of payments to scene painters, and opera libretti
contribute many names. Scene painters were less highly
regarded than on the Continent and were seldom acknowledged in playbills or advertisements until the time of De
Loutherbourg in the 1770s. The emphasis was not on the
décor but on the play and the actors. Advertisements tanta-
lisingly refer to new scenes and dresses but their creators are
anonymous. When the names of four painters were put on the
playbill of Thurmond's *The Miser*, 1727, Theobald condemned
the innovation as a modern affectation.[44] Yet some scene
designers were eminent as, for example, James Thornhill,
decorator of St. Paul's and Greenwich Palace, and Francis
Hayman, well known for his conversation pieces and his
decorations at Vauxhall. Painters in the early part of the
century were often also decorators of stately homes or public
buildings. They did not confine their activities to scene painting, nor were they regularly employed at the theatres. But they
also on occasion decorated the playhouses, as when Hayman
and Oram worked on the ceiling paintings at Goodman's
Fields, Cipriani on that of Covent Garden and Marinari on

44. Dedication, *Rape of Proserpine*, 1727.

the ceiling, proscenium and box panels at Crow Street, Dublin. Artists and draughtsmen were engaged as scene painters, as in the case of Nasmyth in Edinburgh, Malton, an architectural draughtsman, and William Hodges and Charles Catton, both topographical draughtsmen, in the patent theatres.

The popularity of Italian opera resulted in the engagement of Italian and foreign scene painters, mostly at the King's Theatre. The first to come was the young Marco Ricci and a companion, probably G. A. Pelligrini, in 1708–1709. They were followed by Roberto Clerici, who had been both scenographer and machinist in Vienna. The great Servandoni, when young, supplied seven scenes for operas at the King's, and later returned at the height of his fame. In 1724–1725 a Frenchman, Joseph Goupy, and a Fleming, Pieter Tillemans, were appointed scene designers at the King's and were followed by well known Italians, Jacopo Amigoni, 1729, and Antonio Jolli, 1744–1748. The names of Mittermayer, Bigari and Conti, Münch, Colomba, Waldré and Cipriani stand witness to the continued influx of foreign artists. They brought with them the experience of the great era of baroque scenery in Continental centres and, though nothing of their work here is extant, they undoubtedly kept the English stage in the main stream of development.

The first painters to be attached to a theatre were John Harvey and George Lambert at Lincoln's-Inn-Fields, the former from 1724–1725, the latter from 1726–1727.[45] Both moved with Rich into Covent Garden in 1732 and painted new scenes for that theatre. John Oram was house painter at Drury Lane from 1747–1748 to 1758 and was succeeded about 1763 by John French. Both Oram and French belonged to families of scene painters, the first we hear of in England. Scene painting had become a profession where father trained son to succeed him. Numbers and salaries rose steadily: by 1767–1768 we find two scene painters and four assistants (who

45. Dates follow theatrical seasons, which ran from October to June.

undertook such routine jobs as renovating stock scenes) at Covent Garden; by 1785–1786 the number had risen to ten, and by 1794–1795 to twenty-seven, though not all these were regulars. At Drury Lane ten is the largest number recorded in one season.

There were three types of employment: (1) regular house painters engaged by the season at a fixed salary; (2) assistants or apprentices usually paid by the day; (3) painters paid by the piece for a particular production. Remuneration varied according to experience and management, but salaries were lower than those of actors. Servandoni was one of the highest paid, receiving 600 guineas for a winter season at the King's. De Loutherbourg claimed as much, but Garrick refused to pay him more than £500. Greenwood senior earned £646 for thirty-two weeks' work at Drury Lane in 1792. In the last years of the century, when several painters were employed, the weekly bill at Covent Garden was about 16 guineas. These figures are evidence of the growing importance attached to the scenic department.

There is little evidence as to how the work was divided but, arguing back from 19th century practice, it is probable that, when several new scenes were provided for a new play, each was allocated to a single painter with his assistants. Thus Acts I and III of *Lodoiska*, 1794, were assigned to Greenwood and assistants and Act II to Malton and his assistants, Lupino and Demaria. This would give homogeneity to each scene but a variety of styles to the whole piece. De Loutherbourg introduced a different division of labour—that between designer and executant. He made only models from which French, Greenwood or Royer painted the actual scenes. O'Keeffe explains how the décor was planned: 'a copy of the drama is put into the hands of the artist who is to plan the scenes . . . he considers upon it, makes models in card-paper, and gives his orders to the painters. The author is often brought into the scene-room to give his opinion of the progress of the work' and the wardrobe keepers were supplied with a copy to enable them to produce suitable costumes.[46] O'Keeffe has omitted the manager, who certainly had a large say.

A watercolour by Michael Angelo Rooker depicts him at work on a scene in the Haymarket Theatre.[47] He is using a scene frame which, on a system peculiar to England, was let down through a slot in the floor so that the upper portion could be reached. No cradle, by which the painter could be raised or lowered, is evident, but one was installed at Covent Garden in 1788.

Opera and Pantomime

There is a little more illustrative material for the 18th century than for the Restoration but, even so, it is scant enough in comparison with that of the Continent. Where are the scene designs and sketches by De Loutherbourg once owned by Garrick, or the 380 models and drawings listed in the De Loutherbourg sale? Of actual scenery there is no trace and, if we want to see whole sets in action, we have to go to Drottningholm in Sweden or to Cèsky Krumlov in Czechoslovakia. We had no small court theatres where scenery was preserved and it could hardly survive in the rough and tumble of the repertory system in the public theatres. Nor were funds available for the kind of lavish commemorative volumes that princelings issued. The first decades of the 18th century were dominated by the craze for Italian opera. From the beginning it was associated with spectacular scenery as its predecessors, the dramatic operas, had been. Like them, its themes were based on neo-classical and Ovidian fables, to which were added heroic plots from Tasso.

The Queen's (later the King's) Theatre, built by Vanbrugh, opened in 1705 and shortly provided the opportunity, as it was large and unsuitable for the spoken voice, for housing Italian operas, until in due course it was used almost exclu-

46. *Recollections*, 1826, Vol. 2, p. 36.
47. British Museum. S. Rosenfeld, 'A Georgian Scene-Painter at Work', *British Museum Quarterly*, Vol. 34, Nos. 1–2.

sively for this purpose. Three months previous to the opening
of the Queen's with an Italian opera, Clayton's Italian style
composition, *Arsinoë*, had been presented at Drury Lane.
James Thornhill was commissioned to design four new scenes,
for which we have his drawings. The first is a garden with two
pairs of asymmetrical wings and a back scene of a fountain
and is inscribed 'by Moonlight' (Plate 11). The second is a
room of state with statuary. There are three pairs of wings,
again asymmetrical with cut out arches parallel to the proscenium on one side, whilst on the other a *trompe l'oeil* effect
suggests a lateral scene at right angles to it. This may have
been an alternative suggestion for the wings, though it is
hardly likely that they were lateral as the drawing suggests.
The back scene is an alcove with side niches and a painted
drapery border to mask the top. The third is a hall with three
pairs of matching wings of cut out, coupled columns leading

PLATE 11. James Thornhill, *Arsinoë*. Garden scene by moonlight.

through an arch to a garden. Lastly, another garden scene with three pairs of tree wings has a perspective back scene of a parterre with a haven and ships beyond. The back scenes are widely designed and their perspective is not based on a vanishing point geared to the seat of a king, but, as befitted a public theatre, was sufficiently horizontal for a good part of the audience to see it all. The scenes are remarkably simple and their style classical rather than baroque. However, Thornhill designed at least one baroque scene, a great flat scene for an unknown piece.[48]

The advent of Italian designers for the opera provided it with scenery in the Italian manner. Ricci, though a Venetian, had a very different style from that of the magnificent Torelli, if we are to judge by his scenic sketches at Windsor.[49] He rejected the sumptuous baroque in favour of a lighter and more naturalistic manner, in which he may have been influenced by Juvarra. A German visitor remarked of his work for *Hydaspes*, 1710, that 'the scenery and properties had all been made expressly for the opera and were very fine, though not so costly as those in Italy'.[50]

Aaron Hill, however, was not impressed. In his Preface to *Rinaldo* he complained that Italian operas were 'wanting the Machines and Decorations which bestow so great a Beauty in their Appearance' and on this account were seen to disadvantage. As manager of the Queen's Theatre he hoped to remedy this by filling the eye 'with more delightful Prospects'. Hill was a reformer with high standards of presentation and he attempted to carry out the elaborate scenes and effects required by his libretto for Handel's opera. The opening scene of walled Jerusalem besieged and part of a camp is reminiscent of Webb. Among the scenic effects were a chariot

48. Art Institute of Chicago. Reproduced, Southern, Plate 29. *Arsinoë* drawings are at the Victoria and Albert.
49. Reproduced, A. Blunt and E. Croft-Murray, *Venetian Drawings at Windsor Castle*, 1957.
50. Conrad von Uffenbach, *London in 1710*, ed. W. H. Quarell and Margaret Mare, [1934], p. 18.

drawn by dragons emitting fire and smoke; a grove with flying birds; a black cloud descending filled with spitfire monsters; a calm sea with mermaids dancing in the water and a boat sailing out of sight; steep mountains rising from the front of the stage to the utmost height of the most backward part with rocks, caves and waterfalls, and the blazing battlements of an enchanted palace. The mountain was climbed by actors and opened to swallow them up, then vanished, revealing a rock in the middle of the sea which ascended; lastly came a view of open country with Jerusalem at the side built on a rock with a practicable winding highway by which the army stormed the city. *The Spectator*[51] debunks all this: 'An Opera may be allowed to be extravagantly lavish in its Decorations . . . Common Sense however requires, that there should be nothing in the Scenes and Machines which may appear Childish and Absurd. How would the Wits of King Charles's Time have laughed to have seen Nicolini [the singer] . . . sailing in an open boat upon a Sea of Pasteboard? painted Dragons spitting Wild-fire, enchanted Chariots drawn by *Flanders* Mares, and real cascades in artificial land-skips . . . Shadows and Realities ought not to be mix'd together in the same Piece and . . . Scenes which are designed as the Representations of Nature, should be filled with Resemblances, and not with the Things themselves'. This interesting passage not only suggests that design had declined, but carefully distinguishes between illusion and reality, rejecting the latter as well as the unhappy yoking of the two. Yet the cascade was popular enough to be seen again in *Clothilda*, where it helped to keep the house cool!

Expensive new scenery had to do service for succeeding operas. Thus *Pyrrhus and Demetrius*, 1710, took over scenes from *Almahide* and in turn Clerici's palace scene for *Pyrrhus* was on view again in *Cleartes* the following season. *Theseus*, 1713, which was presented with four new scenes, decorations, machines and rich habits, promptly bankrupted Swiney, the

51. March 6, 1711, No. 5.

manager, who decamped without paying for them.

Some years after *The Spectator's* onslaught, in 1727–1728 the fine quality of operatic scenery is mentioned by a Frenchman, De Saussure. He remarked on the frequent changes of scenes and decorations, 'some of them being of rare beauty'.[52] A few years later Francis Colman characterised the scenes and clothes for *Orlando Furioso*, 1733, as 'extra-ordinarily magnificent'.[53] If we are able to judge by Thomas Lediard's design for his *Britannia*, Haymarket, 1738, we must endorse these views. Lediard, when in the diplomatic service, had made a magnificent series of designs for the annual celebrations of the English King's anniversary in Hamburg.[54] *Britannia* too was a piece of the celebratory type beloved of the baroque stage. For it Lediard devised what he calls a 'transparent theatre', illuminated and embellished with machines in the full baroque manner (Plate 12). The setting was a Temple of Honour, of which the pillars were transparent. Behind the open arches of the cut backcloth can be glimpsed a triple perspective. A cloud machine bearing Mars and Peace has descended and later another was to follow with Jupiter and a third, filling the whole back of the stage, with an assembly of gods. This is the most Torellian design we have for an English production and it was a triumph for a small theatre.

Of the foreign painters who worked on the operas, Giovanni Servandoni was the most famous. Probably he succeeded Clerici as scene painter at the King's in 1721, when a young man. After a long spell in Paris as director of the Paris opera and organiser of spectacles at the Salle des Machines, he returned to London in 1747 and worked for Rich at Covent Garden. Two years later he designed scenery for Handel's *Alceste* at the King's, but the opera was abandoned. One of his scenes—the palace of Pluto, said to be a noble design— was got out from store for a revival of *The Rape of Proserpine*

52. *A Foreign View of England in the Reigns of George I and II*, 1902, p. 272.
53. Opera Register, B. M. Add. Ms. 11,250.
54. R. Southern, 'Lediard and Early 18th Century Scene Design', *Theatre Notebook*, Summer 1948, Vol. 2, p. 49.

PLATE 12. Thomas Lediard, *Britannia*.

twenty years later. The same or another scene, the Palace of the Sylphs, was seen in *The Sylphs* in 1774. Several of his Continental scene designs are extant, but we know of none that he did for London. It is significant that one of the leading baroque scene painters of his day thought it worth his while to work here.

Another Italian, Michael Novosielski, who was an architect as well as a scene painter, settled in London and, after working for a short time at Drury Lane, was engaged as a scene painter and machinist at the King's in 1781. He reconstructed Vanbrugh's original theatre the following year, converting the auditorium into a horseshoe shape. He was appointed master painter in 1783 with three assistants and designed operas and many of Noverre's ballets until 1784–1785, when he was succeeded by Marinari. Such was the rivalry between the two men that they are said to have painted out each other's scenery. When the King's burnt down in 1789 Novosielski was engaged to rebuild it and returned there as painter and machinist until his death in 1795.

Gaetano Marinari worked as scene painter and machinist on the operas from 1785 until 1794 and so was the scenographer for the first productions of some of Mozart's operas. His practicable hell for *Don Giovanni* was much admired for the effect of fire produced by means of transparencies. After Novosielski's death, he worked both for the King's and Drury Lane and he made alterations to the interior of the former in 1796. He was employed there on and off until 1808, when he was succeeded by Aglio. He lived to be over 80 and ended his days in poverty. Planché considered him inferior to De Loutherbourg and condemns his unnatural blue trees; Raymond, on the other hand, says he was accounted one of the first scene painters in Europe and Gilliland mentions that he had a classical mind and produced some of the finest specimens of architectural scenery.[55] Though nothing remains of his work or Novosielski's, there can be little doubt that it was at the opera that the neo-classical traditions survived.

The great success of John Rich's pantomimes in the 1720s meant that the patent theatres had to provide elaborate scenery for them. The first part was usually based on myths; the second transformed the deities into *commedia dell'arte* figures, and Harlequin and Columbine danced through a rapid succession of localities. Elaborate machinery and frequent changes were required. Theobald claimed in the Dedication to his *Rape of Proserpine*, 1727, that pantomime did not, like opera, need the importation of expensive foreign singers and so could better afford artistic settings and machi-

---

55 .*Era Almanack*, 1874, p. 65; G. Raymond, *Memoirs of Robert William Elliston*, 1844, Vol. 1, pp. 175–176; T. Gilliland, *Dramatic Mirror*, 1808, Vol. 1, p. 160.

nery. Between 1722–1723 and 1729–1730 eleven pantomimes were staged with new scenes.

John Devoto was the scenographer concerned with those at Drury Lane, Lincoln's-Inn-Fields and Goodman's Fields. Like many of his predecessors and contemporaries, he started as a decorative painter. A book of his sketches in the British Museum, and one or two more finished designs, are in the full baroque tradition (Plate 13). Some of the sketches are adaptations from Juvarra and Pietro Righini, two of the outstanding Italian scene designers of his day, and show how carefully he studied their work. He experimented with the *scena per angolo*, or diagonal perspective, which may have been invented by Juvarra and was exploited by the Bibiena family, who dominated 18th century scenography. Whether any of these designs were used in his productions we do not know; if so, they were more ornate than one would expect for the pantomimes. Devoto's scenes for *Harlequin Student* at Goodman's Fields included a baroque style view of Elysium with bowers and flowers and a heaven of heathen gods descending, which may possibly have been based on the drawings. He also made a set of scenes of ancient Rome for *Julius Caesar*, Drury Lane, 1723, the earliest record of scenery for Shakespeare, which may have been in grander style.

The young George Lambert made his name with spectacular scenery for *The Rape of Proserpine* at Lincoln's-Inn-Fields, 1727. The alternation of mythical with grotesque scenes was reflected in the mingling of palaces, gardens, heaven and hell with domestic scenes of a farmyard, country house and chamber. Pantomime inherited baroque machines and Ceres's palace falls in an earthquake and Mount Etna erupts through the ruins. In the final scene the heavens open and Pluto and Proserpine once again rise from hell. The stage in four sections with eight wings and four borders, listed in the Covent Garden inventory, was used to achieve such effects. What was new was the trick scenery devised for Harlequin's escapes or for the sudden transformations of props. Thus in *Harlequin*

PLATE 13. John Devoto. Unidentified setting.

Sheppard, 1724, the escape involved tearing down shutters and leaping through a window and ceiling. The magic bat of Harlequin effected its transformations by means of a flap hinged to the scene. A wing was divided horizontally, one

71

half scene above, another below. The flap which completed
the lower scene was attached above and, when it fell, revealed
its reverse side, which completed the top half which its fall
had discovered. These flaps are familiar from 19th century
toy theatre designs. De Saussure was impressed by the
decorations and machinery of the pantomimes. He describes
how bushes appeared out of rocks and grew into trees, so that
the stage resembled a forest in which flowers bloomed, 'the
most surprising and charming picture you can imagine'. The
barrel, groove and weights for these trees, which were raised
through a slot in the boards, are listed in the Covent Garden
inventory.

This theatre, built by Rich in 1732, was supplied with
mechanisms for raising whole stages. For *Harlequin Sorcerer*,
1752, 'the whole Stage with the scenery and all about it,
rises up gradually' in the air, a motion similar to that used in
The Prophetess in 1690 (Plate 14).

Pantomime continued to be the chief purveyor of elaborate
scenery and machinery throughout the century and much of
the painters' energies were absorbed in getting up these shows
every season.

Scenery for Plays

The décor for plays lagged behind until the time of Garrick.
Much of it was stock, by its nature generalised. It might give
a sense of period, classical or Gothic, but rarely depicted a
particular place. Stock palaces in classical style served for *Zara*
in Jerusalem and *Artaxerxes* in Persia (Plate 15). Dr. Southern
contends that stock scenery has an aesthetic merit since it was
conceived not as illustration but as stylised decoration, but
this savours of making a virtue of necessity. Because it was
familiar it did not distract attention from play or players. The
view that play scenery should not be too obtrusive is expressed
by the author of *The Actor*, 1755: 'we should not have the
scenes of a play like those of an English pantomime, or an
Italian opera; because we would not have them engross that

72

PLATE 14. George Lambert, *Harlequin Sorcerer*. Farmhouse scene.

attention which is more due to the player. . . . The changes
must not be violent or many, but there must be some. Even
where the conduct of the play does not require it, the imagination of the audience does, the eye is tir'd of the sameness
though it be proper'. He cites the dissatisfaction of the
audience with Garrick's revival of *Phaedra and Hippolytus* where
unity of place was observed by only one scene. Aaron Hill,
on the other hand, regarded 'decoration . . . however slighted,
or ill-understood among us'[56] as essential, and he backed his
opinion by supplying at his own cost new scenes, decorations
and dresses for his *Fatal Vision*, 1716, and *Henry V*, 1723. Few
authors could afford this luxury and had to be content with
new dresses and one or two new back scenes at best, accompanied by stock wings. Dr. Southern has calculated that the

56. Dedication to *Fatal Vision*.

73

Covent Garden inventory, 1744, lists only nineteen sets of wings as against forty-three flats. Wings then often remained unchanged in front of different back scenes. Complaints were made that a merchant's counting-house was staged with a palace colonnade enriched with pillars and statues at Smock Alley, Dublin, in 1771,[57] but such inconsistencies were usually accepted as normal practice.

A substantial part of the scene painter's labour went to freshening and renewing the stock scenes which suffered a deal of wear and tear in the extensive repertory. Replacements were sometimes distinguished by their artists' names, such as 'Dall's Hall' or 'Harvey's palace'. Successive painters designed new variations on the old themes and audiences could compare various palaces, gardens or prisons. An Irish writer reduces necessary stock scenes to temples, tombs, city walls and gates, exteriors and interiors of palaces, streets, chambers,

57. *Hibernian Magazine*, April 1771, p. 145.

prisons, gardens and rural prospects of groves, forests and deserts.[58] To these one might add castles, camps, seashores and caves.

New scenes were sometimes provided for new plays. Samuel Johnson's *Mahomet and Irene*, 1749, was granted 'scenes splendid and gay such as were well adapted to the inside of a Turkish seraglio, the view of the gardens belonging to it was in the taste of eastern elegance', an early attempt to create an oriental atmosphere. Ten years later Garrick embarked on a policy of providing more scenery for new plays and revivals. He started with *Antony and Cleopatra*, 1759, with new scenes, habits and decorations, which did not save it from failure. In 1761 he had new scenes for *Cymbeline*. A German visitor that year was impressed by 'the quantity of different decorations, machinery and dresses'.[59]

Garrick returned from a two year sojourn on the Continent in 1763 determined to improve Drury Lane's scenic department. A series of new plays with new scenery by French was produced. Professor Burnim reckons that Garrick provided nineteen new sets for thirty-seven legitimate dramas, and that by the time he retired in 1776 he was spending six times as much on scenery and painters' salaries as at the outset of his management.

Foreign visitors testify that standards in the London theatres could compare to those in Europe. Grimm in 1774 found the decorations lavish, the effects dazzling, the changes as frequent as demanded. Ten years later Watzdorf considered scenery, costumes and lighting at both theatres magnificent, while Brandes recorded that the scenes were the best he had seen 'not gaudy opera decorations but realistic productions of actual scenes'. The fine library scene for *The School for Scandal* is a good example (Plate 16); to be noted are the masking drapes and the paucity of furniture. In this realistic field England was a pioneer.

58. *The Case for the Stage in Ireland* [1758], p. 35.
59. J. A. Kelly, *German Visitors to English Theaters in the Eighteenth Century*, 1936, p. 30.

PLATE 16. *The School for Scandal*. Library scene.

Topographical and Architectural Scenery

Topographical pictures were popular in the 18th century and this taste was mirrored on the stage. Topographical draughtsmen, such as Charles Catton and Thomas Malton, found employment in the threatres. As the century progressed more localised scenery was painted and this was accompanied by a demand for greater accuracy of presentation. We have seen that London places of fashion were depicted in Restoration comedies and this trend continued, whilst more out-of-the-way views were seen in opera and pantomime. In 1707 a front prospect of Blenheim Palace, then being built by Vanbrugh, was shown at a celebration of Marlborough's victories at the Queen's Theatre.

Two follies, the Hermitage and Merlin's Cave, had been

erected in Queen Caroline's garden at Richmond and were shown by Devoto at a revival of *King Arthur* at Goodman's Fields in 1735. Not to be outdone, Covent Garden arranged a pantomime, *The Royal Chace, or Merlin's Cave*, round these popular follies. Such English views catered to the pleasure of recognition. The volcano vogue, started by Lambert in 1727 with a scene used again in 1769, was taken up by Garrick, who countered with two new scenes of Vesuvius at Drury Lane in 1771: 'the first of which represents a Vulcano [*sic*] burning at a distance, and is reflected by the water in the bay of Naples. The second is a nearer land view of the Mount, and represents the manner in which the Lava is thrown out whenever an eruption happens; the torrents of the lava, like a river of liquid fire, falling into a cascade from a rock'. A writer objected to 'those Mummeries in which the carpenters, painters and taylors belonging to the theatre are the principle projectors'.[60] The delight of spectators in representational scenes is mentioned by Roger Pickering in 1755: 'If the *Streets, Buildings, Rooms* and *Furniture, Gardens, Views of the Country*, &c. be executed in the *Tast of the Country* where the Scene of Action in the Play lies, and the *Keeping* and *Perspective* be *good* the whole House never fails to give the most audible Evidence of their Satisfaction'. Later he adds: 'there should never be such a *Scarcity of Scenes* in the *Theatre*, but that, whether the Seat of Action be *Greek, Roman, Asiatic, African, Italian, Spanish*, &c., there may be one *Set*, at least, adapted to *each* Country'.[61]

The passage shows the growing trend towards realism and authenticity. Algarotti in his *Essay on Opera*, 1767, went further, urging scene painters to read about the places they were depicting and to converse with men skilled in the customs of antiquity. He asked them to study the architecture of Greece and Egypt and the gardens of China as well as

60. *London Stage*, Vol. 4, p. 1596, quoting *Theatrical Review*, December 26, 1771.
61. *Reflections upon Theatrical Expression in Tragedy*, 1755, pp. 59, 76.

contemporary buildings. The inclusion of Chinese gardens reflects the taste for rococo *chinoiserie*, which Garrick and Noverre imported from Paris in the ill-fated *Les Fêtes Chinoises* in 1755. Boquet, whose earliest known commission it was, was engaged for both decorations and costumes. The wings were furnished with balconies filled with painted Chinese figures.[62] This was followed by Murphy's *Orphan of China*, 1759, with new scenes. When this was presented at Crow Street, two years later, Carver painted a new set of scenes 'in the true Chinese taste'.

The basing of scenery on actual sketches drawn on the spot started as far back as 1724 in the topical pantomime, *Harlequin Sheppard*, which included scenes of Newgate, Drury Lane and Clare Market. Dall and Richards were sent to Stratford in 1761 so that their scenes for *Man and Wife or the Shakespeare Jubilee* should be authentic, and Richards visited Windsor in 1768–1769 before painting scenery for *The Institution of the Garter*. These were *pièces d'occasion* but at Sadler's Wells in 1790 scenery for two pieces about the French revolution, painted by Greenwood and Pugh, were copied from accurate drawings or descriptions by people specially appointed to attend ceremonies in Paris.

In the provinces and in Ireland local scenes grew in popularity. Bamford and Jolly supplied a set of landscapes, including Killarney, O'Sullivan's Cascade and the mountains of Glena, for *Harlequin in Ireland*, Smock Alley, 1773, thus anticipating De Loutherbourg's Derbyshire pantomime. Tate Wilkinson in York employed a local topographical draughtsman to paint scenes of York Minster and Castle Howard for his pantomime in 1779, and in Manchester in 1780 Banks provided a set of local views for another pantomime. Since the scenes had to be recognisable to local audiences a degree of faithfulness to the originals is implied. These scenes are the most distinctive contribution to scene design of provincial theatres, whose

62. Bert O. States, 'Servandoni's Successors at the French Opera', *Theatre Survey*, 1962, Vol. 3, p. 46.

managers were for the most part content to copy scenery from London.

Michael Angelo Rooker (Plate 17), the Haymarket scene painter, 1779–1794, was one of those commended for accuracy: 'The distinctions of situation, time, costume, and architecture, so rarely attended to by the painters at the winter theatres are here observed with critical exactness'.[63] Correctness of architectural detail was also a speciality of Thomas Malton, employed at Covent Garden and Drury Lane, 1781–1796.

PLATE 17. Michael Angelo Rooker. Unidentified garden scene.

His father was the author of *A Complete Treatise on Perspective*, 1775, who believed that 'It is the least qualification of a scene painter to be excellent in landscape, in which a small knowledge of perspective is prerequisite; but in order to execute designs in architecture with correctness, and a just proportion of the several parts, requires a thorough knowledge of perspective', and this study should be the basis of the scene painter's art. When Drury Lane was in course of rebuilding in 1793 Malton painted a scene of the scaffolding, which changed to an exterior of the theatre as it would be on completion, considered a great credit to his architectural talents.

This is a far cry from the idealised fantasies of the baroque, though Jones, Webb and Stephenson occasionally produced views of particular localities. Accuracy is coupled with mastery of perspective, whose illusionist quality was beginning to be trained on the representation of actual places.

Innovations and Experiments

Before the time of De Loutherbourg there were no radical innovations in settings in the 18th century, but there were some improvements which rendered staging more flexible. There were more built up pieces in addition to the ascendable mountains and habitable arbours used by Jones. Aaron Hill devised a practicable bridge for his *Henry V*, Drury Lane, 1723, on which the opposing French and English kings entered with a barrier between them; the accompanying courtiers had to wait below as the bridge held limited numbers. The tomb in *Romeo and Juliet* for Garrick and Miss Bellamy was a large built up chamber filling half the stage. The mill in Inigo Richards's scene in *The Maid of the Mill*, 1765, (Plate 18) worked and a girl is shown seated at an open window. A similar practical window is seen in a print of *The Padlock*, 1768. These were part of the scenery, which replaced the windows above the proscenium doors of the Restoration. Juliet's balcony is also listed in the Covent Garden inventory as a separate piece. The use of practicable doors in the scene

80

PLATE 18. John Inigo Richards, *Maid of the Mill*.

also increased. Tate Wilkinson writes of a flat with two folding doors in the middle which was in use at Covent Garden
in 1747. These served as new points of entrance for the actor
and the dramatic effect of flinging them open was exploited
in the melodramas of the 1790s.

A few experiments were made with the placement of wings.
Aaron Hill speaks of 'slanted scenes' which were to be set
back as far as possible for his *Merope*, 1749. He seems to have
reverted to the old Italian method of placing wings obliquely
instead of parallel to the proscenium. More important is the
occasional use of lateral flats running towards the back scene
instead of parallel with it. Dr. Southern's reproduction of the
print of *The Padlock* clearly shows a narrow back scene

81

flanked by two raking flats with one pair of wings in front. Odell drew attention to an interior scene at the Haymarket of similar type. The play illustrated (Plate 19) is *Three and the Deuce* which is located in an inn hall with three doors leading to three named chambers. The side walls of these two scenes were half way to a box set, but there is no evidence that they were completed by a ceiling cloth.

The 18th century saw the development of the drop scene, which descended on rollers as an alternative to the back flat in two parts. Apart from the great curtain in *The Prophetess*, 1690, Odell found the first mention of one for a revival of *Harlequin Sorcerer*, Covent Garden, 1752: 'a scene drops and gives us a prospect of ruinous rugged cliffs, with two trees hanging over them beautifully executed', by Lambert. At Drury Lane in *The Genii* the same year a scene dropped

PLATE 19. *Three and the Deuce*, showing lateral flats.

'containing a rural prospect which exceeds any landskip yet shown on the stage . . . the reapers enter, the scene rises and leaves them in the field'. The inventory of Crow Street, 1776, includes a drop wood and a drop palace. By the time Kemble opened his new Drury Lane in 1794, all the back scenes for *Macbeth* were lowered from the flies. The drop scene had this advantage for the scene painter: his painting no longer had to be cut in two and joined in the middle, leaving a visible vertical line. Drops were not widely used until the 19th century, when they gradually ousted flat shutters. W. J. Lawrence, however, estimated that it was not until about 1890 that the last pair of flats was 'consigned to the limbo of the unwanted'.[64] In our conservative theatre they had a long run.

The principle of dropping scenes from rollers was soon found to be serviceable for act drops. Curtains had been occasionally used for this, but drops could be painted with landscapes, townscapes or classical ruins for the audience to enjoy before the play opened or during the intervals. Odell traces the act drop to 1754 on the Dublin stage, when riotous spectators slashed a finely painted one. Garrick used a landscape drop for *Cymon*, 1766, and this was probably used again for *Alfred*, 1773, as the prompt book specifies 'Drop Landskip after Acts I and II'. Carver's first work for Garrick was a famous drop which depicted a storm on a coast with the sea dashing against the rocks, according to Edward Dayes 'the finest painting that ever decorated a theatre'.[65] Act drops were not confined to a particular play and some, like De Loutherbourg's for *The Wonders of Derbyshire*, continued in use for some years.

It was at the Haymarket for *The Red Cross Knight*, 1799, that a drop was first used to mask a scene change, still customarily made in public. It met with disapproval on the grounds that 'this method of preparing for a new scene disjoints the business,

---

64. *Stage*, March 6, 1930, Vol. 1, p. 116. The article is unsigned.
65. *Works*, p. 323.

and of course tends greatly to injure the effect' as well as causing delay.[66] All the same, drops eventually came to be used to conceal changes. More than anything else on the perspective stage they resembled easel pictures on one plane and thus were part of the shift from the architectural to the pictorial style.

A new scene shifting system was introduced at a few theatres. It had been invented by Torelli, who used it at the Teatro Novissimo, Venice, in 1641. By means of a barrel and shaft mechanism all the scenes could be moved simultaneously by ropes instead of by hand manipulation. It was installed in the new Lincoln's-Inn-Fields and for Theobald's masque of *Decius and Paulina*, 1718, 'the Scenes and Machines [were] after the Venetian Manner'. Some of the elaborate changes were described as having been achieved 'in twinkling of an eye'. The system was in use in Covent Garden as the inventory lists a scene barrel as well as smaller ones for raising trees and for Banquo's trap. When Chetwood went to Smock Alley in 1741 he engaged a machinist from one of the London theatres 'who alter'd the Stage after the Manner of the Theatres in *France*, and *England*, and formed a Machine to move the Scenes regularly all together.'[67] Though pronounced a masterpiece of mechanism, it was a failure and had to be abandoned. It was not re-introduced there until the stage had been refloored in 1774, but thereafter was in constant use. When a similar machine was installed in the new Crow Street Theatre in 1758 it was announced that the stage was the same height as that at Covent Garden and 'framed in such a Manner as to admit Machinery never attempted in this Kingdom, and is to be furnished with 20 different views of Scenes, which may be shifted in less than one minute by one Man only'.[68] This system was a great asset, whilst the wing and back cloth arrangement lasted, but was defeated

66. *Morning Chronicle*, August 22, 1799.
67. *General History of the Stage*, 1749, p. 73.
68. *Faulkner's Journal*, January 31–February 4, 1758.

eventually by the box set and built up pieces.

Some progress was made in lighting even before De Loutherbourg. Garrick inherited the hoops of candles hung over the stage (Plate 15) which could be drawn up when a dark scene was required. When the stage had to be darkened for the opening scene, as in *The Tempest*, the candles were not lighted until later. Garrick's innovations were the result of his tour abroad, but we cannot be quite sure what form they took. 'Taking away the candle rings, and lighting from behind—the only advantage we have discovered from Mr. Garrick's tour abroad', wrote one acid commentator.[69] Garrick abolished the hoops, which hung indiscriminately over landscapes and streets, and he must have replaced them by improved lighting behind the wings. He installed a new type of batten for the lamps there with reflectors which could be swivelled to obtain graduations of light for various times of day. Jones had, however, already been capable of atmospheric nuances.

A further advance towards subtlety was made by Angelo senior, who had seen a model theatre in Venice in which the scenes were transparencies and figures in profile were moved behind them. He constructed a similar model, which was admired by Gainsborough and other landscape artists. Garrick asked him to contrive such a scene for *Harlequin's Invasion*, 1759, which French painted with opaque wings but a transparent back cloth, behind which visionary figures flitted with the effect of enchantment. Screens were placed diagonally covered with scarlet, crimson and blue moreen (not the customary oiled silk) with a powerful light in front. By turning them towards the scenes the colours were reflected in turn, so that the stage appeared on fire.[70] French repeated the experiment in a view of Ludgate Hill illuminated for the celebration of a victory in 1770.

Garrick also gave attention to the reform of costume in

69. Nicholas Nipclose, *The Theatres*, 1772, p. 11.
70. Henry Angelo, *Reminiscences*, 1828, Vol. 1, p. 13, *et seq.*

period pieces, though productions of Shakespeare and other historical plays were still for the most part dressed in the fashion of the day.

Realism was in the air and Garrick's acting was more natural than the declamatory style of his predecessors. This was accompanied by a movement away from the idealisations and architectural grandeurs of the baroque towards a simpler and more everyday type of staging. The baroque played magnificent variations on a few themes for the glorification of princes. Though this *raison d'etre* faded with the Hanoverian dynasty, the style lingered on in Italian opera and in some pantomimes. After a century and a half its formalities were out of tune with the times. The unity of atmosphere which Inigo Jones had created was lost in the public theatres. With mixed scenery, some old, some new, some fine, some tatty; with scenic settings divorced from the periods or climes of the plays, a singleness of impression could hardly be expected. Yet some splendour was retained for 'beautiful', 'magnificent', 'dazzling', were terms that could still be used by foreign visitors. The demand for spectacle is always with us, but after the first seventy years of the century even spectacle underwent a radical change from the architectural to the pictorial. It was De Loutherbourg who triggered off the high romantic revolution on the stage.

CHAPTER VI

The
Romantic
Movement

Philip De Loutherbourg

De Loutherbourg, who had previously been employed in Paris and worked under Italian painters, was engaged by Garrick in 1771 as scene designer at Drury Lane. As an artist he was influenced by Salvator Rosa, and his easel paintings were in thorough-going romantic style; he gloried in wild landscapes, picturesque effects and dramatic lighting. Burke had published his work on *The Sublime and Beautiful* in 1756 and his concepts had become familiar, both in England and abroad—the time was ripe for them to be translated into scenery. The romantic has a particular appeal to the English temperament, nurtured not on the sunshine and clear skies of the south but on mists and nuances of light, creating an atmosphere of mystery. De Loutherbourg conceived his settings as pictures rather than as architecture; his perspectives were no longer the formal ones of the Italian style but were broken up in a more natural fashion, and it was owing to his work here that England became a pioneer in romantic scenery and for the first time led, and did not follow, the Continent.

De Loutherbourg set out his ideas in a correspondence with Garrick.[71] He explained that he wished to invent new effects which would involve altering the theatre's lighting system

71. Copies in Forster Collection, Victoria and Albert.

87

and method of scene shifting, and installing new machinery. He would make models from which carpenters, painters and machinists could work and he offered to design the costumes and supervise the execution of the scenery by the house painters, the decorations, machinery and lighting. He insisted on complete control of the visual side of the productions. The designer thus became the artist responsible for creating a unified stage picture, harmonising the diverse elements under one directing hand, a conception not realised since the days of Inigo Jones.

De Loutherbourg achieved the breaking up of perspectives which had held the stage for so long by the greatly increased use of separate pieces. The rigid back flat and wing system was modified by the introduction of raking pieces supported by braces which could be set at various angles. Juvarra had placed his flats on different parts of the stage as early as 1708–1712 and Servandoni had introduced the method into France in 1728. England had been constricted by the groove system of setting and changing scenes which, because of their permanent positions on the stage, had not allowed for flexibility. De Loutherbourg did not abolish the grooves but 'by introducing bits as cottages, broken stiles before the flat he gave the whole a stronger resemblance to nature'.[72] He made much greater use of ground rows to fill the empty central spaces between the wings, as can be seen in the print of *A Christmas Tale* (Plate 20). It has been stated that in *Omai* he used as many as forty-two separate pieces to represent a frozen ocean.[73]

De Loutherbourg's other main reform was in lighting, which enabled him to create much subtler transitions than hitherto and to add to the range of effects (Plate 21). French and Angelo had preceded him with the technique of throwing tints on to the scenes through transparent material. De

72. Pasquin, *Memoirs of the Royal Academicians*, 1793, p. 77.
73. 'Historical Sketch of the Rise and Progress of Scene-Painting in England', *Library of Fine Arts*, May, 1831, p. 328.

PLATE 20. Philip James De Loutherbourg, *A Christmas Tale*.

Loutherbourg's method was to use coloured silks on the side scenes with lights which, when pivoted, illumined the wing behind. These 'newly invented transparent shades' shed 'a vast body and brilliancy of colour' on the scenes with an enchanting effect. In *A Christmas Tale*, his first pantomime, the audience was struck by a sudden transition of forest foliage from green to blood colour. Gainsborough, who had approved of French's colours, complained to Garrick that these were garish and begged him to 'maintain your lights, but spare the poor abused colours till the eye rests and recovers'.[74] Since, however, he recommended sticking to red, blue and yellow he seems to have objected to the constant change rather than brilliance of colouring.

74. J. Forster, *Life and Times of Oliver Goldsmith*, 1854, Vol. 2, 345 n.

PLATE 21. Philip James De Loutherbourg. Maquette of prison scene.

De Loutherbourg also used gauze and is credited with inventing an effect of Harlequin in a fog by hanging dark veils in front of him. Gauze was certainly in use for the ballet of *Orpheus and Eurydice*, Kings, 1785, where in an Elysian Fields scene 'a filmy hue is thrown over the stage, and figures assume the appearance of aerial beings'.[75]

Another innovation of De Loutherbourg's was the use of

75. *London Stage*, ed. C. B. Hogan, Part 5, p. lxvi.

small models or cut outs which passed across the stage and were moved mechanically. In *Alfred*, 1773, his first production, complete models of ships by the marine painter, Serres, took part in a naval review. Even more ambitious in *Queen Mab*, 1775, in a scene of a Thames regatta, barges were rowed to music, each oar keeping a regular stroke. In Sheridan's *Camp*, 1778, battalions of figures marched out in order.

Under Garrick, De Loutherbourg provided more new scenery for new plays instead of concentrating on the pantomimes. From 1774 to 1776 he supplied scenery for six plays and afterpieces and two pantomimes; under Sheridan, 1777–1782, for ten new plays and five pantomimes. All we have left are a few incomplete maquettes in the Victoria and Albert Museum. The sale catalogue of his designs lists some 380 pieces, including 49 general, 23 rural and architectural and 26 cloud and water. Other subjects were military, marine, infernal, gardens, rocks, moonlight, waterfalls, camp, prisons, caverns and conflagrations.[76]

The key piece for De Loutherbourg's landscape revolution was the pantomime, *The Wonders of Derbyshire*, 1779, which was based on views of that county. He made preliminary sketches on the spot for the scenes. The piece opened with an act drop of mountains and waterfalls 'most beautifully executed, exhibiting a terrific appearance'.[77] Of the whole scenery Angelo goes on to say 'never were such romantic and picturesque paintings exhibited in that theatre before'. Eleven of the twelve scenes were localised, the last being a transformation to a palace and gardens. The majority were landscapes and two were caverns. Different times of day were represented, such as Matlock at sunset, Dovedale by moonlight, and another landscape at daybreak. De Loutherbourg often displayed his lighting effects in this way. One writer

---

76. *A Catalogue of Drawings of James Philip De Loutherbourg*, sold by Peter Coxe, June 18, 1812. Victoria and Albert Library. I owe this reference to Dr. Joppien.
77. H. Angelo, *Reminiscences*, Vol. 2, p. 248.

adjudged the settings superior to any since those of Servandoni 'with several advantages in the disposition and illumination'.[78] The touchstone of naturalism was beginning to be used by critics. One, after praising the views of Buxton Wells and Poole's Cavern as 'taken with great exactness', expressed reservations about the view of Castleton in which the entrance was 'too much beautified and illumined'.[79] Again writing of *The Runaway*, 1776, a critic says that De Loutherbourg was: 'The first artist who showed our theatre directors that by a just disposition of light and shade, and critical preservation of perspective the eye of the spectator might be so effectually deceived in a playhouse as to take the produce of art for real nature'.[80] It was no longer the miracles wrought by machines that roused enthusiasm, but truth to nature.

The romantic passion for the exotic was also catered for. *Sethona*, 1774, had an early example of an Egyptian setting; *Electra* a Greek one; *Robinson Crusoe* a Spanish. A south sea islands décor was used for *Omai*, Covent Garden, 1785. The pantomime was based on Captain Cook's voyages and the scenery was adapted from drawings and prints by John Webber and William Hodges who accompanied him on the expedition. It was executed by a team of painters, including Richards, Carver and Hodgins. The nineteen scenes were mixed English and tropical, as customary in pantomime. Among the latter was a royal burial place by moonlight, Otaheite at sunset, the Sandwich Islands, the rocks and native habitations at Kamtschatka and a witch's cavern which was set on fire.

Further possibilities of scenic display were explored by De Loutherbourg in his model theatre, the Eidophusikon, exhibited in various rooms, 1781, 1786, 1787. On a stage only 6 feet wide and 8 feet deep the artist contrived five scenes interspersed with four transparencies. The latter underwent

78. *London Packet*, January 8–16, 1779.
79. *London Magazine*, January 1779, p. 31.
80. Quoted by Russell Thomas from *Morning Chronicle*, February 17, 1776.

repeated changes by the operation of modified light on their transparent and semi-transparent surfaces, and by the intervention of opaque and coloured materials. Thus, in the scene of Milton's hell, the colours changed to a sulphurous blue, a lurid red, a pale light and finally 'to a mysterious combination of the glasses, such as a bright furnace exhibits infusing various metals'. For the Greenwich scene the transition was from 'the cool hue of verdure which appears at dawn to the refulgent warmth of the blushing morn'.[81] The sun's reflections on water and moonlight were greatly admired. De Loutherbourg thus succeeded in producing atmospheric transitions within a single scene instead of by a succession of scenes. For greater brilliance of lighting he made use of the recently invented Argand lamp, which was first installed in the theatre at Drury Lane in 1785. In order to display clouds rising from the horizon at various speeds De Loutherbourg stretched painted linen on a frame twenty times the size of the stage and raised it diagonally on rolling cylinders. This technique is illustrated in an Italian watercolour of about 1750[82] which also suggests that he may have obtained his effects of great distance in perspective by the use of a series of ground rows.

Wave machines turning on spindles and varnished to reflect lightning, sound effects of thunder, waves and rain, all added to the illusion. The great popularity of this show influenced scenic work in the theatre and revealed new techniques and methods for increasing the illusion of reality. Other results of De Loutherbourg's work were to enhance the value accorded to the scenic side of the production, to increase the number of scenes for plays, and to put scene painters on the map. Henceforward their names appeared more regularly on playbills and advertisements, a recognition long overdue.

81. W. H. Pyne, p. 303; *Whitehall Evening Post*, March 1, 1781.
82. Gascoigne, fig. 189.

Landscape Scenery of John Inigo Richards and Thomas Greenwood

Covent Garden had a landscape tradition from the two artists, George Lambert and Nicholas Dall. Dall was the link between Lambert and Richards, with whom he worked from 1765 to 1776. Unfortunately nothing is left of his work. Richards was scene painter at Covent Garden from 1759 to 1803. He painted many kinds of scenery, particularly for the pantomimes, which at this theatre attracted most of the new mountings. For instance, he collaborated with Cipriani on a Tartarus scene for *The Mirrour or Harlequin Everywhere*, 1779 (Plate 22). This, though displaying the customary background of flames and torments of the damned, is no match

PLATE 22. John Inigo Richards and Giovanni Battista Cipriani, *Harlequin Everywhere*. Tartarus scene.

for the grandeur of baroque hells. More original was his typical rustic mill scene for *The Maid of the Mill*, 1765, (Plate 18). In contrast to De Loutherbourg's wild landscapes, this is a peaceful English scene and displays that delight in nature and peasant life which was another hall mark of the romantic movement. We also know that Richards painted scenes of a country church and a farmyard with hedge and hayrick.

When it came to exotic scenes, Richards had preceded De Loutherbourg in copying drawings to illustrate views, in this case Asiatic by Tilly Kettle, for *The Choice of Harlequin or the Indian Chief*, 1782. For Indian buildings and landscapes for

PLATE 23. Inigo Richards, *Ramah Droog*.

Ramah Droog he adapted drawings by Thomas Daniells (Plate 23). This placid design makes a slight atmospheric attempt at exotic trees and demonstrates the use of ground rows. When Richards supplied a frontispiece for Covent Garden in 1784 it was said to resemble an easel painting which lacked a frame,[83] and thus aimed at the pictorial rather than the architectural.

Thomas Greenwood the Elder was at Drury Lane from 1772 to his death in 1797 and became that theatre's chief resident scene painter after French's death, whilst in the summer recess he worked at Sadler's Wells. He executed a good many of De Loutherbourg's designs and painted scenery for pantomimes and the melodramas which were just beginning to come into fashion. One of the first was Burgoyne's *Richard Coeur de Lion*, 1786, for which there was a castle scene in wild mountain country and another of the inner works of an old fortification, of which we have an engraving. Once again the perspective is broken up by set pieces, a forecourt of the prison and a walled platform, whilst behind is a drawbridge not centrally situated. Some of Greenwood's landscapes were engraved for the scores of the comic operas: a camp on the Danube in *The Siege of Belgrade*; the bay of Naples in *The Pirates*, from views taken on the spot by the composer, Stephen Storace, and a moated castle in a park for *Lodoiska*. These are local views, but for the pantomimes he returned us to the fairy world of enchanted gardens, magic fountains, rocks opening to display a ship sailing away and tacking about, and an oak which put forth leaves and then withered. At Sadler's Wells, where Greenwood collaborated with Andrews, scenery varied from the high romantic view of Fingal's Cave as described by Pennant to the storming of the Bastille.

Greenwood was succeeded by his son, Thomas, by whom we have an engraving for the melodrama *Blue Beard*, 1798. It is a complete hotch-potch of western and oriental architectural styles represented by a pile of built up pieces.

83. G. Saunders, *Treatise on Theatres*, 1790.

Gothic melodrama, which came in with Monk Lewis's *Castle Spectre*, 1797, started a vogue for gloomy vaults, castle halls and Gothic chapels. Forty years after Walpole had initiated the taste for the Gothic in his *Castle of Otranto* it reached the stage in the painted architecture of the melo-dramas.

William Capon and Antiquarianism

Henry Holland reconstructed Covent Garden in 1792 and rebuilt Drury Lane in 1791–1794 as theatres of a much larger capacity than hitherto. Drury Lane held 4,000 and was the biggest in Europe, the opening for scenery was 43 feet wide and 38 feet high, whilst the backstage was vaster, 83 feet wide, 108 feet high and 92 feet long.[84] At Covent Garden the forestage was still 20 feet long, the same as the original Drury Lane. Such immense stages needed a great deal of scenery to make an effect particularly built up pieces, which had to be shifted mechanically from above and below. The scenery from the old Drury Lane did not fit, so that J. P. Kemble was free to start from scratch and he chose Capon, who shared his passion for the medieval, to design much of his scenery. The painter took infinite pains to reproduce remains of actual buildings 'with all the zeal of an antiquary'[85] and his sketch book[86] illustrates the meticulous care with which he worked on drawings of the Tower or Westminster, noting the type of stone or material used in their construction and marking the lights and shadows. From these sketches he designed scenes for appropriate plays: the Council Chamber, Crosby Hall, for *Jane Shore*, 1814; the Tower restored for *Richard III*; and for a Gothic Library in *The Iron Chest* he copied the vaulting from St. Stephen's, Westminster.

Capon designed a Gothic chapel for Kemble's opening oratorio which resembled 'a Gothic cathedral with illuminated

84. For details, see *Survey of London*, Vol. 34.
85. J. Boaden, *Memoirs of the Life of John Philip Kemble*, 1825, Vol. 2, p. 101.
86. In possession of Mr Francis Watson.

stained glass windows'. He replaced the borders 'which hung like so many tattered remnants' by ones 'carved like a fretted roof in an antique pile' and removed the wings for 'a complete *screen*, like those in use at the foreign theatres, thereby perfecting the deception of the scene'.[87] Though orchestra and singers were within the set it can hardly be accounted the first box one. Lateral screens were indeed employed but there is no evidence that the roof was a painted cloth, anyway the scene was not for a play which required entrances. Capon also provided stock scenes of New Palace Yard and the Palace of Westminster. Later, when Kemble moved to Covent Garden in 1809, he painted six wings of old English streets and twenty pairs of flats selected from archaeological remains, of which two designs are extant (Plate 24).

Kemble planned a series of Shakespeare revivals with new settings and dresses for the re-opening of Drury Lane in 1794. For these he employed not only Capon but a team of scene painters, including Greenwood, Malton and Catton. For *Macbeth* there were some fifteen new scenes with a drop curtain by Malton. This latter seems to have been used to conceal scene changes, as a critic grumbled about the ludicrous 'perpetual curtain'. Kemble also reformed the costumes, though here his antiquarianism was selective. The production was spectacular but some effort was made to give it an authentic period flavour.

The huge stage and machinery which had been installed enabled Capon to build up a great Gothic scene for Baillie's *De Montfort*, 1800. It represented a 14th century church with nave, choir and side aisles in seven planes about 56 feet wide, 52 feet deep and 37 feet high. If these figures of Boaden's are correct and are compared with Holland's measurements for the stage it becomes evident that the scene used neither the whole length of it (92 feet) nor the width (83 feet) but must have been chiefly placed in the back stage of 83 feet as the front was only 43 feet. A writer who styled himself 'An Artist

87. *Thespian Magazine*, March 1794, p. 127.

PLATE 24. William Capon, ancient street for stock scenery.

and An Antiquary' comments: 'The Artist, at great pains and labour, followed the style of building of the fifteenth century among us, and, by an ingenious contrivance, gave practicable side ailes [*sic*], and an entrance into a choir, &c., whereby, the spectator, for a short space, might indulge his imagination to believe he was in some religious pile'.[88] The fact that this scene was later used for a Gothic Hall shows the limits of Kemble's efforts at authenticity. In a series of articles, 'Of the Impropriety of Theatrical Representations', the above critic condemned a number of antiquarian gaffes and incongruities, as, for example, the intrusion of an open battlement inside a

88. *Gentleman's Magazine*, May 1801, pp. 408–409.

Saxon tower, or, even worse, a Gothic chamber whose folding doors were surmounted by a pediment. He denounced 'some slight observations made from our national architecture in a way that most artists think quite sufficient for the purpose of bringing specimens of ancient splendour before the eyes of the publick'. The demand for a much stricter standard of authenticity was to bear fruit in the work of Planché and Charles Kean. Nevertheless, we must accord Kemble acknowledgment for trying to introduce settings more in keeping with the plays and for replacing the old and worn stock scenes that had hitherto been deemed good enough for Shakespeare by fresh settings designed for specific plays. The desire to recreate past eras, especially in the medieval style, was one of the symptoms of romanticism which Capon and Kemble translated on to the stage.

More Shakespeare Revivals

Kemble continued his Shakespeare productions at Smirke's new Covent Garden from 1809 after Drury Lane had been burnt out. Once again he opened with *Macbeth* with scenery by a team of painters, Grieve, Phillips, Whitmore and Lupino. The pre-eminence of Shakespeare in Kemble's thought was visually acknowledged by the drop of a temple dedicated to the dramatist, including his statue in Westminster Abbey. Scenery, machinery, costumes and decorations were praised for their general effect and particular detail. *Lear* was treated to a vaguely Saxon setting but, as one critic remarked, 'A manager is not to be pinned down to rigid propriety'. In the season of 1811–1812 eight Shakespeare revivals were staged with varying degrees of scenic success. *Henry VIII* was appropriately Gothic and its spectacular possibilities were siezed on. *Coriolanus* was praised for the sculpturesque beauty of its Roman architecture, even though it was the Rome of the Caesars and not of the Consuls. The tendency to make spectacle an end in itself was on the increase and pantomime effects and elaborate pageants were staged at the expense of the texts. In *The Tempest* the order of scenes was sacrificed to preparations for the shipwreck which occurred in Act II. *Antony and Cleopatra*, with Egyptian scenery by Phillips, Pugh, Hollogan and Whitmore, was given a spectacular sea battle in which the huge galleys got in the way of the combatants, producing 'unwieldy and unpicturesque confusion'. *The Examiner* bitterly criticised the presentation of a fragmented Shakespeare for the sake of this fight, a funeral procession, and in *Coriolanus* 'a paltry imitation of a Roman Triumph, though as much like one as it is like a Lord Mayor's show'. This did not deter Kemble from staging *A Midsummer Night's Dream* with a triumph of Theseus, a scene of clouds descending and opening, fairy royalties in chariots and other remnants of baroque splendours. Thus started that succumbing to spectacle which was to bedevil Shakespeare productions for a hundred years.

After Kemble's retirement Elliston continued to try to stage Shakespeare beautifully at Drury Lane, where his painters were Marinari, Andrews, Hollogan and Dixon. Marinari staged the storm in *Lear* after the manner of the Eidophusikon; the coloured screens rotating before the lights gave a supernatural tint but played on Edmund Kean's face with shifting hues, whilst the noise effects swamped his voice. There was a sea with tumultuous billows, creaking boughs of trees on which each leaf hung separately and rustled, as well as 'every infernal machine that was ever able to spit fire, spout rain, or make the thunder'.[89] Elliston considered it absurb to confine himself to Saxon architecture, which he thought would be of too rude construction, but he was careful to announce that decorations and costumes were authentic and based on facsimiles of engravings.

The coronation of George IV was the occasion of an elaborate pageant of Henry V's coronation in a revival of *Henry IV*, 2. Authorities were duly consulted and Dixon

89. C. Murray, 'Elliston's Productions of Shakespeare', *Theatre Survey*, November 1970, Vol. 11, p. 2.

reproduced the scene outside Westminster Hall with tiers of painted spectators, and the interior of the Abbey with all the ceremonial appurtenances was painted by Andrews and his son. Real horses were brought on for the champion, a preview of equestrian drama.[90]

Meanwhile at Covent Garden worse was happening with what Leigh Hunt denounced as the 'lyrification' of Shakespeare. Frederick Reynolds made an operatic holiday out of a series of comedies also produced for their spectacular potential. The Grieves, Pugh and Hodgins the younger were responsible for the scenery. Among these mummeries was the injection of the masque of Ceres and Juno from *The Tempest* into *Twelfth Night*, 1820. Leigh Hunt, however, acknowledged the beauty of the scene, which reminded him of Inigo Jones. *The Two Gentlemen of Verona* was treated to a carnival in Milan, Cleopatra's galley sailing down Cydnus, and an artificial mountain in the Duke's gardens which exploded to discover a temple of Apollo. This was a reversion from antiquarianism to baroque, but two years later the reaction came.

J. R. Planché, an antiquarian and authority on costume, persuaded Charles Kemble to stage *King John* with authentic dresses, for which he would be responsible.[91] This production in 1823 was a landmark. J. P. Kemble had consulted the antiquarian, Douce, but had refused to go the whole hog for fear of being thought an antiquarian himself. His brother, Charles, swept this half-hearted reform away 'with an attention to Costume Never equalled on the English stage'. He set the fashion for quoting his authorities in the playbill. The lack of new scenery was remedied in *Henry IV*, *1*, though it was the costumes that still caught the attention. For *Cymbeline*, 1827, the three Grieves painted views, as accurately as stage effects would permit, of the 'Buildings of the Gaulish and Belgic colonists of the Southern Counties of Britain before

90. C. Murray, 'Elliston's Coronation Spectacle, 1821', *Theatre Notebook*, 1971, Vol. 24, pp. 57–63.
91. *Recollections and Reflections of J. R. Planché*, 1872, Vol. 1, p. 52.

their subjugation to the Romans'. One critic makes fun of this parade of learning: 'We expect next to see legitimate authority produced for the dressing of Puck, and authenticated wings allotted to Mustardseed'. This pedantry may have had its place in ridding Shakespeare production of a ridiculous hotch-potch of styles but it proved a limitation. All this detail was unnecessary even in an historical play and showed more devotion to archaeology than to artistry.

The Grieves

This family dominated scene painting from 1820 to the mid-1840s. It consisted of John Henderson Grieve and his sons, Thomas and William. As the group of painters, Whitmore, Pugh, Hollogan and Hodges, at Covent Garden dropped out the three Grieves became jointly responsible for most of the scenery and they made the theatre renowned for its mountings. For a brief spell, 1835–1839, they transferred to Drury Lane, but returned to Covent Garden under Vestris until 1843. After the deaths of William in 1844 and John in 1845 Thomas carried on the tradition to become the leading painter for Charles Kean. More of their designs are extant than for any other scene painters: over 600 at the University of London Library and another 100 or so at the Victoria and Albert and British Museums. We may therefore assess their style more easily than that of their contemporaries.

It ran the gamut of the romantic picturesque: mountains and torrents, ruins by moonlight, burning forests, oriental temples and palaces, Gothic abbeys, and illuminated cities, gardens and ballrooms. Their colouring could be both brilliant and subtle; they were masters of perspective and of light and shade. Edward Fitzgerald accounted them 'the most perfect scene painters in the world as a combination' and they raised the standard both of design and execution. They exploited the use of cut scenes, through which perspectives were seen, and of transparencies and gauzes for the creation of luminous and soft lighting. Though they introduced the panorama on to 103 the stage they were not outstanding innovators technically and continued to work with the back scene, wing and border system varied by built up pieces, profiled and cut scenes, and set scenes behind the back scene. They may have been the first to use the sink and fly device by which the scene was divided horizontally, the upper half being flown and the lower sunk through a cut in the stage.

A good many of their designs were for opera and ballet, then at the zenith of their popularity. It was the period when Scott's novels were staged and the Grieves provided scenery for them from *Rob Roy* in 1818 to a *Kenilworth* ballet in 1832 (Plate 25). They also executed scenes for *A Vision of the Bard*, Sheridan Knowles's masque in tribute to Scott. The sketch for the scene of Dryburgh Abbey by moonlight has a set piece of his tomb, which descended down a trap to allow of a series of tableaux from the novels managed by invisible strong lights. Byron's *Manfred*, 1834, was another highlight of the romantic age, for which a new stage was laid down. Among the Grieves's scenes were those of the Jungfrau with its glaciers and an avalanche.

The annual pantomime gave opportunity for magical fantasies and for travelogues. Nearly thirty countries are represented in their designs, including many exotic ones such as Java, Peru, Tartary and the South Seas.

The Grieves and their contemporaries enjoyed the new benefit of gaslight, which was introduced in 1817. Leigh Hunt describes how 'Their effect, as they appear suddenly from the gloom, is like the striking of daylight, and indeed it is in its resemblance to day that this beautiful light surpasses all others. It is as mild as it is splendid—white, regular, and pervading'.[92] Every part of the stage could now be seen with equal clarity and it was calculated that the volume of light was equivalent to three hundred Argand lamps. The advantage to the scene painter was not only in the steadier, less

92. *Leigh Hunt's Dramatic Criticism*, ed. L. H., and C. W. Houtchens, 1950, p. 153.

PLATE 25. William Grieve, ballet of *Kenilworth*. Banqueting hall by moonlight.

flickering, light but in the ability to control the amount of illumination on the scenes; times of day and nuances of atmosphere could be more easily suggested. We must imagine this new brightness and these nuances on some of the Grieves's brilliant spectacles. For *Cherry and Fair Star*, 1822, they devised a grove with myriads of beautifully plumaged birds in motion and a burning forest in which the whole scene appeared ignited. Their limitations were evident in a sea scene, where the surge beating against the city towers was accomplished by the ludicrous, if traditional, method of boys, at a shilling a head, tumbling under a sheet of canvas. For the final transformation to the Bower of Bliss a mirror flat was placed midway on the stage, which reflected both the auditorium, the fairy dance and the cupids in mid-air—a novel device.

The thirteen scenes for the world première of Weber's

Oberon, 1826, are said to have cost £6,000. Several were of oriental splendour but most admired were the transitions from sunset to twilight, starlight and moonlight over a seascape. Crabb Robinson enjoyed it as a fine show: 'the paintings are magnificent and for the greater part in very fine taste—The machinery, flying cupids, sea nymphs and aerial cars approach the perfection of the French Opera and the Milan Theatre de la Scala'.[93]

One of the highlights was the masked ball in Auber's *Gustavus the Third*, which was brilliantly illuminated and contrived to appear larger than it was. It was exceeded in depth and altitude by the illuminated salon in Auber's *Lestocq*, supported by forty transparent crystal columns. Some of the garden and grotto scenes have a delicate, fairylike quality and an enchanting beauty of perspective.

The Grieves were not wedded to archaeological exactitude, though on occasion they quoted authorities, referring to Ker Porter for the scene of Persepolis in *Artaxerxes*. They also reproduced easel paintings on the stage, such as Venet's picture of Napoleon taking leave of his companions in arms and West's of Charles II landing at Dover. This is evidence of how pictorial scenery had become; the painters aimed to create a picture in three dimensions. The Grieves were more romantic than realistic, and comment concentrates on their qualities of beauty and picturesqueness rather than on their verisimilitude. They could reconstruct a classical scene when the work demanded, as in Rossini's *Siege of Corinth*, but it was mainly in their panoramas that they produced recognisable views.

Panoramas. David Roberts and Clarkson Stanfield

The panorama was invented by Robert Barker, an Edinburgh artist, in 1787 and he displayed it successfully in 1795 in a hall. The diorama, invented by Bouton and Daguerre, was

93. *The London Theatre, 1811–1866*, ed. Eluned Brown, 1966. Society for Theatre Research.

first shown here in Regent's Park in 1823. It achieved a three dimensional effect by painting two pictures on transparent surfaces, one behind the other. In the theatre the terms seem, however, to have been interchangeable. The Grieves first introduced the panorama into the theatre in *Harlequin and Cinderella* in 1820 on a revolving transparency. The same year for the Christmas pantomime they rolled a back scene across the stage from one cylinder to another with a succession of marine views as a background to a ship crossing the Irish Channel. Thereafter the panorama became a regular feature of the Christmas pantomime.

Movement was thereby introduced into scenery at a time when the movement of scene changes in public was gradually being replaced by act drops and drop scenes. English, and later Continental, scenes were the earliest subjects, but in 1823 the Grieves showed the first aeronautic panorama in a balloon excursion from London to Paris. A more elaborate balloon panorama, where the balloon passed through daylight, moonlight, clouds and back to daylight, was on view in 1840. The Grieves travelled in Holland and Germany making sketches for their panorama of those countries in 1834.

The two other chief scenographers who devised panoramas were David Roberts and Clarkson Stanfield.[94] Both started their careers in the theatre and left it for easel painting. They migrated from Edinburgh to London and worked together at Drury Lane, 1822–1824, where their diorama for *Zoroaster* was 482 feet long. Roberts went over to Covent Garden and painted panoramas there, 1827–1830, continuing to supply scenes, mostly for pantomimes, at that theatre until 1844. For *Il Seraglio* in 1827 he painted a drop curtain depicting a ruined amphitheatre. Nothing remains of his scenic work.

We are a little better off for that of Stanfield, as there are nine drawings for *King Arthur*, Drury Lane, 1834, a design for his diorama for *Henry V*, 1839, and an actual act drop of the Eddystone Lighthouse for Dickens's production of Wilkie

94. *Era Almanack*, 1871, pp. 36–37.

Collins's *Frozen Deep*, at Tavistock House, 1855, one of the earliest pieces of scenery we possess.[95] Stanfield started his career at some of the minor theatres which had sprung up in the early 19th century with burletta licences and which became training grounds for scene painters. Under Elliston at Drury Lane he and Roberts competed with the work of the Grieves at Covent Garden. As Raymond says, 'it was now that the public witnessed evidences of art, of which they had hitherto no conception. The masterly delineations and exquisite effects of these two artists became deservedly the admiration of the whole town'.[96] Stanfield had been in the navy, and his marine scenery was outstanding. A panorama of the adventures of a man-of-war was part of the pantomime of 1825 and a representation of Portsmouth in a gale adorned the next year's show. His diorama for *The Queen Bee*, 1828, opened with sunrise at Spithead and included views of Portsmouth dockyard, Cowes regatta, the Needles by moonlight and Gibraltar. His work was not limited to seascapes and for an equestrian spectacle (horses and dogs had invaded the theatres) he painted an ascent of the pyramids. *King Arthur*, based on a story by Scott, was one of his last works for Drury Lane, 1834, for which he painted a splendid hall for the gathering of the Knights of the Round Table, who on horses borrowed from Astley's later stormed the castle by a ramp ascent.[97]

When Macready became lessee of Covent Garden he persuaded Stanfield to provide him with special scenery. His first work was a diorama with views of North Italy, the Alps and Flanders, on which limelight was used to make the painting more brilliant. This proved too expensive and was not used again until 1851 for *Azael* at Drury Lane and by Charles· Kean for *Henry VIII*, where it spotlighted a scene or character

95. Dickens's House, Doughty Street.
96. G. Raymond, *op. cit.*, Vol. 2, p. 329.
97. George Nash, 'A Grand Chivalric Entertainment', *Victoria and Albert Museum Bulletin*, October 1965, p. 4.

and thenceforward was regularly employed. Stanfield's best known work for Macready was his diorama for *Henry V*, which accompanied the words of the chorus, thus rendered superfluous. The English fleet was given visual presentation on its way to Harfleur, the pictorial melted into the action of the siege in a skilful transition and the 'vasty fields of France' were depicted with the opposing camp fires by moonlight. A strikingly dramatic, if dark, design conveys the atmosphere of desolation after the battle (Plate 26). Henry's triumphal entry into London was seen as well as heard. N. P. Willis admired the tableaux and considered that the King's voyage

PLATE 26. Clarkson Stanfield, *Henry V*. Diorama of Agincourt.

and the siege of Harfleur 'were all pictures done in the highest style of art'.[98] Stanfield's last work for Macready was for Handel's *Acis and Galatea*, in which the sea moved towards the audience with breaking waves, spray, foam and the sound of the water as it ebbed and flowed over the sand; and one is reminded of the similar scene by Inigo Jones for *The Masque of Blackness*. Sixteen years later he provided an act drop for Benjamin Webster at the Adelphi which was encased in a painted frame to resemble an easel picture. Stanfield, it is said, taught the pit and gallery to admire landscape and the boxes to become connoisseurs.

Scenic illusion in this period was moving towards realism. Audiences wished to be transported to actual places and periods so that the scene painter's art was concentrated on reproducing the world around him, though frequently seen in a romantic aura, whilst more critics dwelt on how nearly the scenes approached nature and rated them as they would pictures. Only in the pantomimes and ballets was there depicted an escapist, fairy world in which still lingered the illusion of the ideal through spectacular transformations to realms of fancy. Here the imaginations of the designers were given full play.

98. Quoted by Saxe Wyndham, *Annals of Covent Garden*, 1906, Vol. 2, p. 139.

CHAPTER VII

The Victorian Theatre Realism and Spectacle

Domestic realism

The trend towards realism was, in the early part of the century, irregular and sporadic. Tanks of water installed at Sadler's Wells from 1804 for aquadramas,[99] and real horses[100] and dogs in the huge patent theatres for hippo or canine dramas, represented an unhappy mixture of the actual with the simulated. Figures painted on canvas juxtaposed living actors. The way of archaeological exactitude, a form of historical realism, met many pitfalls. Even in mid-century *Julius Caesar* could be produced at Drury Lane in a patchwork of stock Shakespearean backdrops, Roman street wings from *Virginius*, pantomime scenes and an assortment of set pieces.[101] Yet these decades had seen an advance in the care for the visual side of performances of dramas, and romantic realism and antiquarianism tended to give some elements of unity to stage pictures. Domestic settings for comedies had lagged behind. The system of perspective wings was more suitable for palaces than the plain walls of ordinary rooms, where the gaps between the wings were all too evident. Furniture and decorations were painted on the scenery and a minimum of actual tables and chairs was brought on and removed by footmen.

It was Madam Vestris, an actress and manager of refined

99. For these, see *Memoirs of Charles Dibdin the Younger*, ed. George Speaight, 1956, Society for Theatre Research.
100. For these, see A. H. Saxon, *Enter Horse and Foot*, 1968.
101. Prompt book cited by Alan Downer, *The Eminent Tragedian*, 1966.

taste, who reformed all this when she took over the Olympic in 1831. The theatre had only a burletta licence, so was confined to the presentation of pieces with music, such as extravaganzas, comediettas and burlesque light operas. Vestris is credited with the introduction of the box set onto the London stage in *The Conquering Game*, 1832 (Plate 27), but there is no positive evidence in which play it was first seen. Lateral flats had occasionally been used in the 18th century and a full box set was seen in Paris before the 19th century. In 1833 *The Examiner* asserted that Vestris's 'more perfect enclosure gives the appearance of a private chamber, infinitely better than

PLATE 27. *The Conquering Game.* Vestris production.

the old contrivance of wings',[102] but neither this statement nor the evidence of engravings proves the existence of a ceiling cloth instead of borders. Vestris certainly gave verisimilitude to everyday rooms by abolishing the unconvincing wings and by furnishing them with real, not painted, furniture of taste and quality. She took pains to supply good carpets, fine draperies, real blinds over practicable glass windows and props such as clocks, fireplaces, mirrors and even actual door knobs. Such realism was extended to the shop and the garden. The shops in *Burlington Arcade* were built out with transparent windows and had actual goods in them; the windows opened, and showed people moving within, and a lamplighter lit the lamps. In a forest scene a carpet was painted to look like soil and grass and gardens were decorated with real statues and potted plants. The stage was divided into six component parts up which props could be sent, thus minimising waits.

Vestris employed as scene painters William Gordon from Edinburgh, 1831–1834; Tomkins and Pitt to paint stock scenery for operas in 1832; Charles J. James in 1834 and Hilyard in 1835.

In her farewell speech at the Olympic she stated that it had been her aim 'to realise the illusion of the scene by unflinching outlay upon proper costume, and careful attention to the decorations of the stage'. That she succeeded is borne out by the *Theatrical Observer*:[103] 'The mise en scène was never perfect or in good keeping until Mme. Vestris taught her painters how to execute, and the public how to appreciate, her own pictorial conception'. The public did in fact flock to the Olympic to see scenes of contemporary life in close imitations of the drawing rooms and gardens they knew. Vestris created an illusion of reality and imposed a unified conception by the attention she lavished on every detail of the staging. She and her husband, Charles Mathews, continued their work on the vaster stage of Covent Garden, 1839–1842. The Grieves were

102. February 24, 1833, quoted by Waitzkin.
103. April 9, 1842, quoted by E. B. Watson.

their scene painters, and their productions became more spectacular, but they continued to present comedies, such as Boucicault's *London Assurance*, in a style similar to that at the Olympic.

The reforms initiated by Vestris were carried to their apogee by the Bancrofts at the Prince of Wales and Haymarket Theatres. Charles J. James was a link between the two managements and designed scenery for the Bancrofts' first productions in 1865, including a transformation to dreamland in a burlesque *Sonambula*, and a chromatic fountain with limelight effects in *Dame Trot*. He was succeeded by his son, Charles Stanfield James, who had worked with Fenton under Phelps.

The Bancrofts had two advantages: the Act of 1843 had abolished restrictions on minor theatres, and in Tom Robertson they discovered a dramatist whose comedies were expressions of the contemporary taste for realism and could be staged in everyday settings. C. S. James was responsible for those of *Society*, 1865, *Ours*, 1866, and *Caste*, 1867. The attention to detail is evident in the hut scene from *Ours* (Plate 28), though exact realism is here modified by the inclusion of the roof along with the interior. The whole is seen from the outside looking in, rather than from the point of view of the characters. Hawes Craven, later to be Irving's leading scene painter, was engaged for Robertson's later plays and he in turn was succeeded by George Gordon and William Harford, who were responsible for *The Merchant of Venice*, 1875. Bancroft did not approve of changing scenes before the eyes of the audience and so intervals became longer. To minimise these he altered the succession of Shakespeare's scenes, and Gordon painted three carpenter's scenes of Venetian views behind which the set scenes were shifted. One of these was of narrow Venetian lanes 'with their quaint lines of medieval architecture receding in admirable perspective on each side of the fruit-seller's shop in the centre'.[104]

114   104. *Sporting and Dramatic News*, April 24, 1875.

PLATE 28. Charles Stanfield James, *Ours*. Bancroft production.

When in 1878 Gordon and Harford staged *Diplomacy* with four interiors, all solidly built up from carpet to ceiling, this could only be achieved by dint of long intervals. Scenery was becoming too heavily realistic for comfort. The hall in Sardou's *Peril*, 1876, took days to erect and was so strongly built with a massive staircase and gallery that it was impossible to remove it, and a boudoir scene had to be constructed inside it.[105] The long run had become a necessity.

Realism was not confined to the drawing room. For Reade's *Never Too Late To Mend*, Princess's, 1865, Lloyds converted the whole stage into a treadmill, and the most costly scene was 'a perspective of radiating prison-corridors seen from the centre of a model prison, with practicable tiers of galleries, and iron staircases, the cells, and gaslights'.[106]

105. *The Bancrofts. Recollections of Sixty Years*, 1909, p. 217.
106. Henry Morley, *Journal of a London Playgoer*, 1891, p. 313.

The logical conclusion of a picture stage was reached by the Bancrofts at the Haymarket in 1880, when the forestage was abolished and the proscenium surrounded by a gilded frame.[107] The audience was finally cut off from the stage and the players; the world of illusion had retreated within itself. The changeover from back and side scenes to built up structures and enclosed rooms did not come to pass without protest. One critic found that the more complex and elaborate the imitation, the further away was the sense of illusion. The skilfully painted flat had no points of makeshift or weakness, often apparent in built up scenes. Furniture, imported from outside and meant to be seen near to, looked dull at a distance and showed up the poverty of the flat painting, where the walls were at times obviously neither solid nor firm. It was not the case that the closer the reality the better was the effect. Scenery needed to be romantic and exaggerated, larger in fact than life.[108] It was a cogent argument against an overdose of realism.

More Shakespeare Revivals.
Charles Marshall, William Telbin, Frederick Fenton
Macready, when he became manager of Covent Garden in 1837, engaged Charles Marshall and Tomkins as scene painters. Tomkins had worked for Vestris at the Olympic and Marshall had trained under Marinari at Drury Lane. In 1833 Marshall had constructed at the Surrey Theatre the first four room setting on two levels for *Jonathan Bradford*.[109] Such sets had been in use in France and Germany by the end of the 18th century. Though not much employed, they were forerunners of such 20th century examples as O'Neill's *Desire Under the Elms*.

107. R. Southern, 'The Picture Frame Proscenium of 1880', *Theatre Notebook*, April 1951, Vol. 5, pp. 59–61.
108. 'The Limits to Scenic Effect', *Graphic*, December 4, 1869.
109. For prints and details, see M. St. Clare Byrne, 'Early Multiple Settings in England', *Theatre Notebook*, July 1954, Vol. 8, p. 81; G. Speaight, October 1954, Vol. 9, p. 15, for similar scene at Surrey.

Like Vestris, Macready supervised every detail of his productions and aimed at unity of effect. He preferred his designs to represent the atmosphere of a play rather than to stick to pedantic antiquarianism. Thus in *Lear* the castles were heavy and sombre and druid circles rose 'in spectral loneliness out of the heath'. The sensation of power and rude strength dominated a scene in *Coriolanus*, in which precipitous hills beetled over the Tiber, an almost symbolic setting of the drama's theme. The atrium of Coriolanus's house was simple but the view of Antium by night was richly poetic.

The only illustration of Marshall's work is of the wrestling scene in *As You Like It* at Drury Lane in 1847,[110] to which Macready had moved. This filled the entire stage, but the forestage had shrunk to little over 12 feet. A large back drop represented a French chateau on one hand and a landscape on the other with wood and turret wings and a large space of central terrace for the wrestling match. There were ten settings in various grooves and a limited number of three-dimensional pieces. Most of the changes were achieved by withdrawing flats set in front grooves to reveal scenes behind. The only other full scene was the last one of an avenue of beeches. Act drops were used. The stage was still flexible and the waits minimal, enabling Macready to restore a good deal of the text. Birdsong at dawn and the sound of sheep bells added auditory to visual effects.

It will be noted that drops were confined to back and front, or carpenter's, scenes. Flats seldom occupied more than half of the stage, the remainder being devoted to those three-dimensional set scenes which painters and managers regarded as of prime importance. A setting was often judged by the number of set scenes it contained.[111]

Macready engaged William Telbin for *King John*, 1842, his first important commission. Fourteen of his designs were discovered by Professor Shattuck in the Folger Library who

110. In T. H. Shepherd's drawing of Drury Lane. See Shattuck.
111. E. Mayhew, *Stage Effects*, 1840.

reproduced them in his facsimile prompt book of Macready's *King John* alongside Telbin's parallel ones for Charles Kean's production. Both are romantic in style and have obvious affinities. This presentation was most influential and was borrowed from not only by Kean but by Phelps. He strikingly contrasted effects of light and dark, as in his two battlefield scenes, and of massive buildings and open landscape with lighter skies, as in Swinstead Abbey by night. He effectively made use of platforms on three different levels in his scene before the gates of Angis, the top level being slung from the flies. He thus gained an impressive vertical effect. The final scene of Swinstead Abbey by moonlight, with light rendered by blue mediums, was a suitable setting for the King's death, as the gloomy Gothic apartment in Northampton Castle was for the Hubert-Arthur scene. Telbin recreated something of the scene's mood in the setting. For the magnificent roofed throne room which opened the play Telbin used flats set obliquely which crossed the second and third grooves diagonally and ended in a windowed wall in the fifth grooves. *John Bull* took him to task for his colour relationships: Telbin supported blue, which is weak in distemper, instead of red and black, which are strong; his shading was black, which made blue more impure, instead of brown, which would have enhanced it. The waits only totalled eighteen minutes, a tribute to the flexibility of Telbin's technique.

Samuel Phelps, in his great series of Shakespeare revivals at Sadler's Wells, 1843–1862, cut down on the scene changes and mercifully allowed Shakespeare to speak for himself without undue illustrations. Frederick Fenton, who had worked at various minor theatres, was his scene painter. He specialised in the picturesque and set *Macbeth*, 1847, in a rugged mountain landscape. He invented a novel device for the witches, who were placed on a rock back stage behind a green gauze thickened below which obscured them totally when it rose and then they were seen floating in the air, whilst lightning revealed the advancing army. This gauze became a characteristic of Fenton's productions.

Antiquarianism was in evidence, though it was not too laboured. Realistic Egyptian views for *Antony and Cleopatra* were spoilt by Cleopatra's appearance in a fashionable Victorian dress.

Gas was first introduced at Sadler's Wells in *A Midsummer Night's Dream*, 1853. In this outstanding production a diorama with cut wood front scenes and cloud effects behind, which moved simultaneously, was used for scene changes in the forest. A seamless green gauze hung down after the first act, suggesting the hazy atmosphere of a dream, until Oberon and Titania left the stage and day dawned over a pine-clad ravine. Partially painted gauze deepened the effect and provided a visual parallel when Puck was bidden 'overcast the night . . . with drooping fog'.[112] Jerrold says that 'the scenery was quiet and subdued as sylvan scenery at night should be. . . . There are not more than three or four scenes in the whole play, and yet so artistically are the different changes of moonlight, fog, and sunrise produced, that you imagine you have been wandering through an entire forest', and no sounds of scene shifting disturbed the illusion.[113] Fenton achieved with economical means a magical production which outrivalled the elaborate scenery of the larger theatres.

However, elaboration occurred in *Pericles*, 1854. Fenton took the sea as the play's theme and contrived contrasts of rolling billows and tossing ship with a quiet scene in which Pericles appeared to glide along the coast by means of a moving panorama. The trappings of spectacle were perhaps needed to revive this seldom seen play, or Phelps may have been influenced by the early productions of Charles Kean.

Morley summed up the policy of Phelps: 'The scenery is always beautiful, but it is not allowed to draw attention from the poet, with whose whole conception it is made to blend in

112. Southern, *The Seven Ages of the Theatre*, 1961, pp. 254–255, quotes
    Fenton's description from J. Moyr Smith's edition of the play, 1892.
113. Odell, Vol. 2, pp. 322–324.

PLATE 29. Frederick Fenton, *Merchant of Venice*. Belmont. Phelphs production.

perfect harmony'.[114] The beauty is evident in the one design we have for *The Merchant of Venice* (Plate 29).

The Acme of Antiquarianism. Charles Kean

Charles Kean had a personal passion for archaeology and a Victorian passion for education. Both found scope in his productions at the Princess's, 1850–1859. He far outdid his predecessors in his research into period sources, swamped his playbills with details of his authorities, and his stage with splendid mounting and multitudinous period pieces. Macready, after his retirement, wondered whether his lead had not been in some measure responsible for excesses in which 'the text allowed to be spoken was more like a running commentary upon the spectacles exhibited, than the scenic

120   114. *Op. cit.*, p. 129.

arrangements an illustration of the text'.[115] We can visualise the gorgeous pageantry and beauty of setting of some of the productions from a series of water colour drawings of them in the Victoria and Albert Museum.

Frederick Lloyds, William Gordon and J. Dayes were employed on *King John*, 1852, and followed the sequence of Telbin's designs for Macready. Thomas Grieve joined the team, for *Macbeth*, 1853, and George Gordon of the Royal Institute of Architects was consulted on the pre-Norman architecture. Kean was criticised for not providing a more splendid banquet but for representing an 'appropriate feast of coarse fare served upon rude tables, and lighted by simple pine torches' by Dayes. In his eagerness to instruct his audience as to how and where the thanes lived he added a gratuitous scene by Cuthbert of Iona from the mainland. He used the old Davenant-Locke operatic version, his care for authentic Shakespeare being rather less than that for authentic illustration.

Henry VIII was more suitable for Kean's treatment but, as though there were not sufficient spectacular set pieces, he had Grieve paint a panorama of London, copied from a drawing of 1543, in front of which the barges of the Lord Mayor and Council passed on their way to Elizabeth's christening. To give him his due, he restored the vision of Queen Katharine which had not been seen for over a century, and Lloyds brought in a floating stream of angels in limelight. One of them was Ellen Terry, who later recorded her impression of the beauty of the productions in some respect more elaborate than those of her own day. Beautiful, they certainly were, and we have only to look at Charles Fenton's apartment of Queen Katharine with its practical alcove, or Lloyd's spectacular banquet scene with his characteristic diagonal design to realise that the period was splendidly recreated.

Telbin joined the scene painting team for *The Winter's Tale*, 1856, in which the object was to contrast the splendours of

115. *Reminiscences*, Vol. 2, p. 446.

classical Syracuse with the oriental pomp of Asia. So Bohemia was translated to Bithynia. The public was instructed by '*tableaux vivants* of the private and public life of the Greeks at a time when the arts flourished to . . . perfection', and drawings of the props show the meticulous attention paid to every detail from musical instruments to furniture—each item being specially designed. Spectacle was introduced at every opportunity; not only was the pastoral scene a bacchanalian orgy, but a Pyrrhic dance was given at Leontes's banquet. Time's speech was accompanied by an allegorical show by Grieve of classical gods ascending and descending on chariots and clouds dispersing, reminiscent of the masques. It was said to be 'the greatest triumph of art ever exhibited on the stage'. The eye was filled at the expense of the ear and imagination and the art of the painter, not that of the dramatist, took the palm. This production ran for 102 days, thus initiating the long run which led to new scenery for each new play and the gradual disappearance of stock scenery.

Greek settings were seen again in *A Midsummer Night's Dream*. Perhaps Kean had learnt a lesson from the criticism of correct period scenes in *Macbeth* as he abandoned the early time of Theseus as too rude in construction and had the era of Pericles recreated instead. On the opening backcloth the Acropolis was reconstructed by Gordon (Plate 30). The woodland scenes by Grieve, Gordon and Lloyds were enchanting and of a high level of landscape painting and design. They included the habitual diorama by Grieve. One of Gordon's wood scenes was a partial imitation of Turner's Golden Bough and, indeed, Turner's influence is traceable in the luminosity and design of other scenes. Lloyds's final scene had something of a pantomime transformation about it. It was a bold design on two levels with a host of fairies carrying bell flowers descending by flights of steps, whilst rows of figures were painted on the backcloth. Morley saw that the careful reconstruction of the Greek settings was too 'hard and fast' a contrast with the fairy scenes. He has hit on the drawback of this

PLATE 30. William Gordon, *A Midsummer Night's Dream*. Athens from Theseus's palace. Charles Kean production.

type of scenery, in which the overall atmosphere and cohesion of the play was sacrificed to Kean's desire to display classical Athens in all her glory. In the historical plays the archaeological approach did provide a kind of scrupulous unity, but in plays where history was not the theme the approach was inadequate. The scenes were works of art in themselves but inexpressive of Shakespeare's fantasy and comedy.

This also applies to *The Tempest*, 1857, where Caliban was hunted by goblins 'copied from furies depicted on Etruscan vases'. Some idea of the beauty of the lighting effects can be gained by two contrasting water colours of Telbin's scene of an island overlooking the sea. The first (Plate 31) is a brilli-

PLATE 31. William Telbin, *The Tempest*. Storm scene. Charles Kean production.

antly coloured sunrise with a rough sea which abated as the sun rose higher and in the second scene became tranquil with quieter colouring. A desolate perspective by Grieve was conjured into tropical luxuriance by the raising of trees and the gushing forth of fountains and waterfalls—an old but effective device.

Richard II, 1857, had the usual mixture of historically reconstructed buildings and landscapes. It was part of Kean's stagecraft to deploy his actors on different levels, as in the scene of the lists, as well as on ramps and stairways. The centrepiece was a brilliant pageant of Bolingbroke's entry into London, in which the medieval street was crowded with supers.

Similarly in *The Merchant of Venice*, 1858, the Venetian streets with canals, bridges and gondolas were filled with a carnival, a picture of Venetian life in the 15th century 'Not represented as of old, by the traditional pairs of flats of Gothic aspect . . . but the actual square of St. Mark . . . painted from drawings taken on the spot'. Kean was an adept at the grouping and control of crowds, which must nevertheless have cluttered the small stage with its increasingly built up pieces.

King Lear, 1858, of course, had Saxon settings and accoutrements. Another diagonal design was used by Cuthbert for Gloucester's castle, but quite the most original and striking scene was the desolate storm setting by Grieve (Plate 32). This created the atmosphere and can be compared with the open scene for Fechter's *Hamlet* for its low horizon and great sky (Plate 34). Kean's last Shakespearean production was *Henry V*, in which part of the chorus's speech was illustrated by a *tableau vivant* of the English camp with soldiers at prayer. The procession, backed by archaeological authority, was preceded by a ballet of angels in what look very like tutus!

Of the non-Shakespearean productions the most striking was *Sardanapalus*, 1852. Inspired by the Assyrian discoveries of Layard, Lloyds, Gordon and Dayes reconstructed ancient Nineveh. Lloyds's Hall of Nimrod (Plate 33) is a magnificent diagonal design, giving a fine sense of recession and space as it thrusts across the stage.

Morley describes Kean's settings as creating 'out of the theatre a brilliant museum for the student . . . not as dusty, broken relics, but as living truths, and made attractive as well by their splendour as by the haze of poetry through which they were seen'.[116] There is no doubt that as art these designs were outstanding. The composition was often admirable and the lighting, especially for sunrises and sunsets, of a Turneresque brilliance and luminosity (Plate 31). The artists reveal a knowledge of architecture of many periods and a delight in landscape. They worked so well together as a team that one

116. *Op. cit.*, p. 163.

PLATE 32. Thomas Grieve, *King Lear*. Heath scene. Charles Kean production.

can hardly distinguish their individual styles. Considering several were employed on various scenes for one play, and even on occasion on the same scene, the harmony was not impaired. Given Kean's approach, his scenery must have been some of the finest of the century, romantic, realistic and even atmospheric. But scenery is not an end in itself, even when regarded as education, and there can be little doubt that plays and players were often overwhelmed by a mass of conscientious and misdirected detail, and texts were sacrificed to unnecessary pictorial adjuncts and the long intervals neces-

PLATE 33. Frederick Lloyds, *Sardanapalus*. Charles Kean production.

sitated by shifting heavy scenery. Kean was a perfectionist but he was not, like Inigo Jones and Gordon Craig, a visionary.

The Reforms of Charles Fechter

This French actor introduced some radical changes in scene shifting and lighting methods during his management of the Lyceum, 1863–1867. He abolished the grooves, replacing them by the inventions of French mechanists. The stage was remade in sections about 6 feet long and 4 or 5 feet wide which could be lowered to an understage 7 feet deep by counterweights. This was an extension of a system used by J. P. Kemble to raise a pile of scenery from below and by Vestris, who similarly

127

divided her stage. Fechter could preset whole scenes. The scenery was worked in some two dozen slits by upright poles running in tramways below. The poles could be pushed to any part of the stage, in contrast to the rigid positioning of the grooves. Scenery was also flown from a gridiron above, and both curtain and chariot were operated from it by counterweights. The fly and sink system, which had been introduced by the Grieves, had some affinity with Fechter's but it never dispensed with the grooves. Borders were abolished except for foliage and Fechter introduced an early type of cyclorama, thus described by Dickens.[117]

In open outdoor scenes, where, for instance, the open country, or perhaps the open sea, extends far away into the distance, the sky will close the scene in overhead: an unbroken canopy, extending from a certain point behind the proscenium and high above it, over the stage, and away to where, at the extreme backward limit of the theatre, it mingles softly with the horizon . . . this great arched canopy, spanning the stage from side to side, and from front to back, will lend itself to all sorts of truthful and beautiful effects.

From this description it would appear that it was more of a sky cloth overhead than a cyclorama at the back of the stage. A similar contraption had already been seen in the ballet of *Le Corsaire*, Her Majesty's, 1856, when the wings had been withdrawn and an expanse of panoramic sky extended over the stage area.[118]

The gas footlights were placed below the sloping level of the stage. The whole float could be sunk and red or green lights turned up gradually or instantaneously.

Hamlet was Fechter's great role and for the gradual disappearance of the ghost Telbin used Fenton's technique of layers of gauze, with the improvement that they worked on a

117. 'A New Stage Stride', *All the Year Round*, October 31, 1863, Vol. 10, p. 229.
118. Quoted from *Illustrated London News*, July 19, 1856, by M. St. Clare Byrne, article on 'Lighting', *Oxford Companion to the Theatre*, ed. P. Hartnoll.

concealed wheel which caught up fresh pieces of material tinted to match the background until the figure was invisible. Both this and the cyclorama are evident in Telbin's preliminary design(Plate 34). The abolition of the wings has given a sense of spaciousness and of desolation on the empty platform no longer dominated by the usual castle. The settings were Romanesque, and the great hall which filled the stage, with

PLATE 34. William Telbin, *Hamlet*. Battlement scene. Fechter production.

a broad door at the back and a gallery with stairways on each side, was used for most of the action. Fechter alleged that the scenery was not ready in time for the rehearsal and that it had not been properly executed. He refused to pay the full amount of £400 agreed for painting and repairing the scenes. Telbin sued him for the outstanding £136 and won his case.[119]

Fechter's scene painters for the melodramas, which were the staple fare of his short management, were Cuthbert, Dayes and Gates, who had worked with him at the Princess's in 1861. After the termination of his management the grooves were re-installed, to be abolished again, this time for good, by Irving. Fechter's stage had been found to some extent impracticable.

Spectacles and Transformations of William Roxby Beverley

Beverley had his first experience of scene painting in his father's company in Manchester, and his first opportunity to display his gifts under Vestris at the Lyceum, 1847–1855. The extravaganzas of Planché suited his imaginative qualities. He combined pictorial and mechanical talents; these enabled him to develop transformation scenes, which he is incorrectly said to have invented, but in which he excelled. By a new method of going over the cloth while the distemper was still wet, he made himself master of atmospheric effects. He preferred flat to built up scenes as he said: 'Have as much painting as you like, that is legitimate art. A well-painted scene assists the poetry of a drama, for it saturates the imagination; but a built up scene full of elaborate, realistic detail detracts the attention of the spectator from the essentials of the drama'.[120] He also believed that planes should be achieved on a minimum of canvases.

From his career of over fifty years we have only two designs, a backcloth of Brussels for an unidentified play and a sketch

119. Cutting, Enthoven Collection, Victoria and Albert.
120. *Sunday Times*, March 1, 1885, quoted by Emanuel.

for *Henry IV*. Engravings give no idea of his colour and atmospheric effects, though they are witness to the boldness of his designs.

The extravaganzas were based on fairy tales and allied to pantomime, with which they shared elements of fantasy, romance and spectacle. The most famous of Beverley's settings in this field was for *The Island of Jewels*, 1849. A succession of romantic pictures led to one of basaltic caverns in a valley of vapours which dispersed to reveal the crown jewels on the Palm of Success. This transformation was described as 'a Palm Tree in the centre of the stage, the leaves of which unfold, shewing the Blossom . . . which consists of stones of every hue and colour . . . beautiful and goregeous . . . the cupids flying about the air and the rich foliage surrounding forms a complete picture of Paradise'.[121] Planché ensured that the colours of the costumes harmonised with the scenery 'as though they were painting a picture'.

Beverley must have employed painted gauzes for his transformations lit from in front and backed by a dark curtain. The curtain was then raised to discover the set scene behind, and the gauze, when the light from in front of it was removed, became invisible and could be flown unnoticed. This method is in frequent use today.

Like Ben Jonson, Planché in the end resented the supremacy of the scene painter's art. After G. H. Lewes had proclaimed of another basaltic scene 'never on any stage was there such enchantment and artistic beauty', Planché bitterly noted, 'I was positively painted out. Nothing was considered brilliant but the last scene. Dutch metal [a substitute for gold] was in the ascendant. It was no longer even painting but upholstery'.[122]

Beverley's efforts were not confined to extravaganza and pantomime. His shipwreck scene in G. H. Lewes's *Chain of Events*, 1852, succeeded in horrifying George Eliot so much

121. *Theatrical Journal*, January 3, 1850.
122. Quoted by A. E. Wilson, *Christmas Pantomime*, 1934, p. 124.

that she could not look at it. When Beverley became scene painter at Drury Lane in 1854 (and from 1868 exclusively) he designed many Shakespeare revivals, including *Henry IV, 1* for the tercentenary, in which the most notable of his thirteen scenes was that of the battlefield of Shrewsbury, a simple but effective setting in which the combatants in shining armour rose from behind a long ridge and hill with a beacon. *Antony and Cleopatra*, 1873, was mangled to allow for a naval battle, and the description of Cleopatra's barge was given visual accompaniment which, quite unusually, earned the painter a curtain call.

Beverley was addicted to jewelled settings which he used again for *The Doge of Venice*, 1867, in which wheels of glittering gold turned, whilst brilliantly coloured gems were borne up and down in the air.

Boucicault had introduced from America the 'sensation scene', a climax in which violent action coincided with spectacle. For *The Shaughraun*, 1875, Beverley designed the scene of the prison escape. The prison pivoted at the back and disappeared to show the exterior of the tower with Conn clinging to the walls. This ingenious set was pushed by scene shifters in boxes whilst diagonal flats were drawn up. The final scene (Plate 35) consisted of many elements, a solid oblique wall, a rostrum, raking platforms, a cloth pulled forward to cover the stage on the right and a transparency for the bonfire. Though still fundamentally based on wings and back-cloth, the mounting was complicated by a clutter of five set pieces and is an example of the elaboration which had been reached.

Beverley used every means at his disposal. He brought a hansom cab and horse on to the stage; he had moving clouds, and is said to have invented winged ladders with gaslights. By 1881 for *Michael Strogoff* he employed a French type of cyclorama and panorama. But it is above all on the transformations in the Drury Lane pantomimes, which he devised for sixteen years until 1887, that his fame rests. He was

PLATE 35. William Beverley, *The Shaughraun*.

perhaps the most enchanting of Victorian scene painters, as he was certainly one of the most inventive.

Henry Irving's Lyceum Productions

Irving took over the Lyceum in 1878 and ran it for nearly twenty years during which time his outstanding scene painters were Hawes Craven, W. L. Telbin (son of William) and, later, Gordon Harker. Kean conceived of scenery as an illustration to the play, Irving as a setting for the actor's art. He strove towards a unity in which all elements would coalesce to express the mood of the drama and whilst using spectacle, processions and antiquarianism more sparingly than Kean, he sought from his painters primarily beauty and artistry. He employed well known artists to advise on productions or   133 design scenery; for instance Burne Jones designed scenery and costumes for *King Arthur;* Ford Madox Ford designed three scenes for *Lear* in the Roman occupation period; Seymour Lucas directed *Henry VIII* and Alma-Tadema, famous for his classical paintings, designed the scenery for *Cymbeline* and *Coriolanus*. Irving replaced the grooves by flats which could be held by braces in any position. The distinction between wings and back-cloth in the front, and set scene behind, disappeared so that a more simple impression and finer harmony were achieved. He used a black false proscenium for masking so that no longer were breaks in the perspective visible from some parts of the house. The forestage had gone and attention was concentrated on the picture by the lowering of lights in the auditorium. Irving rejected electricity, which was first introduced at the Savoy Theatre in 1881, for the richer, traditional gaslight. The cyclorama enabled Craven to give great space to the skies.

Irving set his tone in his first Shakespeare production. The settings for *Hamlet* were not chosen to display archaeological expertise but to illustrate the text, and the dresses were of the 16th century; 'scenic illustrations in harmony with the poet's ideas', as Irving claimed in his preface. The stage was not cluttered with scenery but beautiful effects of moonlight and glimmers of dawn were visual counterparts of Shakespeare's poetry. For *The Merchant of Venice*, 1879, Craven, Telbin and Hann represented palaces of brick, stone and marble in the Kean style but Irving 'endeavoured to avoid hampering the natural action of the piece with any unnecessary embellishment', and plenty of space was allowed for revelling crowds and the movement of actors. But in *Romeo and Juliet*, 1882, more solidly built up scenes were introduced. The balcony was on marble pillars and Telbin's tomb was of two storeys with flights of steps, gloomy and lit fitfully by lamps. Telbin's famous church scene in *Much Ado*, 1882, had massive, modelled columns, 30 feet high, supporting an ornamental roof. Brereton says 'the figured iron gates, the decorated roof, the pictures, the stained glass, the elaborate and costly altar, the carved oak benches, the burning lights and the perfume of incense, all combine to render this a scene of such richness and grandeur as at first to arrest all thought of the play',[123] which Irving hardly intended. It took 15 minutes to set but it showed Telbin's command of perspective and of atmospheric lighting.

Craven's first sketch for *Faust*, 1886, was realistic but his second idealised. It was mounted in the style of Dürer. Lighting, colour and movement were harmonised, Mephistopheles's scarlet cloak echoing the sunset. Footlights and border lights with yellows, browns and greys emitted artificial sunshine and cool shadows, no longer painted on the scene. Telbin's Brocken had a bleak effect of stormy moonlight in black, white and grey until all was enveloped in a burning mass. Care was taken to have everything of life size in the foreground in order to be in proportion to the figures, whilst the middle and far distance had a proper relationship with the whole.[124] Naturalism was controlled by harmony.

Harker first joined the scenic team for *Macbeth*, 1888. Craven's massive scenes were mounted in 'almost impenetrable gloom' out of which torches flared. Among the seventeen tableaux was one of a gratuitous host of singing witches revelling by moonlight. Irving had not altogether abandoned unnecessary spectacle. His most spectacular production was that of *Henry VIII*, 1892, which rivalled Kean's. A magnificent Tudor Hall by Craven was, like Lloyds's, a diagonal thrust in depth, and the final baptism was set in the Greyfriars' church in Greenwich in splendid Gothic architecture. On it Irving spent £12,000, as compared with only £1,200 for *The Merchant of Venice*. The demand for gorgeous settings had won the day. Alma-Tadema's scene of the Capitol (Plate 36) for *Coriolanus*, Irving's last production, shows the type of classical, architec-

123. *Dramatic Notes*, quoted Odell, Vol. 2, p. 430.
124. Joseph Hutton, 'A Propos of the Lyceum "Faust" ', *Art Journal*, 1886, pp. 24–28.

PLATE 36. Laurence Alma-Tadema, *Coriolanus*. Capitol scene. Irving
production.

tural design he contributed, simple in conception but sumptuous in rendering. The piers at the back were Etruscan and
of monumental quality. The flutings and stripes on them and
on the velarium were white and red, the backcloth a deep
blue sky. Etruscan and Lycian tombs were rifled for the decorations of other scenes.[125]

Irving did not seek to educate his public in history but in
art. He wished to pay tribute to the dramatist by providing
for him a beautiful series of settings, fine in themselves but
also expressive of the play.

125. R. Phené Spiers, 'The Architecture of "Coriolanus" at the Lyceum
Theatre', *Architectural Review*, July 1901, Vol. 10, p. 3.

The Spectacular Tradition. Joseph Harker

Irving's trend towards heavier scenery was paralleled by Beerbohm Tree at his newly built Her Majesty's, 1897–1917. Again plays were cut and intervals extended, which invited reaction against excessive realism and display. Tree had employed Alma-Tadema to design scenery for *Hypatia*, Haymarket, 1892, and he also supervised Harker and Walter Hann's mounting for *Julius Caesar*, 1898. The marble palaces, processions and crowds now provoked criticism for swamping the play; the climate of opinion was changing. The climax was reached in *A Midsummer Night's Dream*, 'stage illusion and stage splendour being capable of nothing further'. A carpet of real grass (legend has it with real rabbits), thickets of blossom, a splendid palace, lights and airy shapes were the components. So magnificent was Craven's garden in *Twelfth Night* (Plate 37), copied from a picture in *Country Life*, that it could not be dismantled and had to remain unsuitably for other scenes or be covered in by front scenes. The system had been carried to self-defeating lengths. Oscar Wilde protested against the displacement of the scene painter by the carpenter: 'the stage is overcrowded with enormous properties, which are not merely far more expensive and cumbersome than scene paintings, but far less beautiful, and far less true. Properties kill perspective . . . the excessive use of built up structures makes the stage too glaring'; some dialogue was 'reduced to graceful dumb show through the hammer and tin-tacks behind'.[126] Against the charge that all had been sacrificed to mounting, Tree contended that his treatment was essential to the proper comprehension of the play!

Harker was the leading realistic scene painter at the turn of the century and during the Edwardian period (Plate 38). Believing that the days of the stock artist were over, he refused to become principal scene painter to Tree and worked as a free lance for most of the managers of his day, including

126. 'Shakespeare on Scenery', *Dramatic Review*, March 14, 1885.

PLATE 37. Hawes Craven, *Twelfth Night*. Garden scene. Tree production.

Alexander, Augustus Harris, Frederick Harrison at the Haymarket, Cyril Maude, George Edwardes and Oscar Asche, as well as on the Empire ballet. His range was wide and he was equally at home in designing classical or medieval settings, elegant suites of modern rooms for Alexander and, later, exotic spectacles for *Kismet*, 1911, and *Chu Chin Chow*, 1916, and *Parsifal*, Covent Garden, with a panorama of the Grail! Harker admitted that there was a tendency to overload Shakespeare but he opposed the taste for green baize curtains. He was not in favour of too many constructed scenes but believed the plays could be performed in full texts by simple and noiseless shifting of painted backgrounds. He was well aware of the problem of combining the real with the artificial:

PLATE 38. Joseph Harker, *Henry VIII*. Banquet scene. Tree production.

'The problems of stage perspective arise from the fact that the artist has a real foreground (the stage) to contend with in addition to what the back-cloth or other parts of the scene may show. The scene has to be designed to look right, or as nearly right as possible, from every part of the house. One's difficulty therefore is that of blending the actual and the artificial in such a way as to make a satisfactory and convincing whole'.[127]

Harker was primarily a perspective illusionist painter, though in later years he had to suffer the influence of 'the reformed school', as in the tercentenary production of *The Taming of the Shrew*, 1916, mounted in a set scene of curtains and screens. To some extent adaptable, he had given thought to the theories of his craft.

Spectacle in the Edwardian theatre found plenty of scope

127. *Studio and Stage*, 1924.

in opera, pantomime, melodrama and musical comedy. The *ne plus ultra* was reached in *The Whip*, Drury Lane, 1909, in which Bruce Smith mounted a horse race on a treadmill (a chariot race had been seen in *Ben Hur* in 1902) and a train wreck (Plate 39). These were enormously admired and the result of great technological skill but they were literally on the wrong tracks. The cinema ensured that for the theatre this kind of realism was a dead end; the moving camera could so far surpass it.

PLATE 39. Bruce Smith, *The Whip*.

CHAPTER VIII

The New Stagecraft

The Precursors

The visit of the company of the Duke of Saxe-Meiningen to Drury Lane in 1881 created a stir, particularly owing to their ensemble playing and management of crowds. But in the latter they had been preceded in London by Macready and Kean, and the Duke himself had been influenced by Kean's productions.[128] The Meiningers broke up mass movements by inventing characteristic actions for individuals. Their scenery was in archaeological style, but was not outstanding. As with Irving, the setting was part of the actors' movements; as with Kean, the stage was broken into different levels and centrality and symmetry were often replaced by diagonal designs. Their importance lay in their stress on an artistic unity of production in which every actor, scene, costume and movement were fused into a total effect.

A similar drive towards an integrated production inspired the theatrical work of E. W. Godwin, the father of Gordon Craig, and led him to insist on the hegemony of a director who would be responsible for every aspect of the production. To some extent this had been done by actor managers, but Godwin went a good deal further as he himself could design both costumes and scenery. He was an architect and, like Planché, an authority on historical costume. He had designed costumes for several managements, and architectural settings

---

128. See M. St. Clare Byrne, 'Charles Kean and the Meininger Myth', *Theatre Research*, 1964, Vol. 3, pp. 137–153; also her 'What We Said About the Meiningers in 1881', *Essays and Studies*, 1965, English Association.

for Bancroft's *Merchant of Venice* and for Wilson Barrett's *Claudian*.[129] They were all in the archaeological tradition but, in addition, he was careful to design colour combinations which would present a unified impression.

Godwin first assumed the role of director for the open-air performance of *As You Like It* at Coombe House. He had entire command over the whole presentation, in which all the arts were co-ordinated. This and the production of *The Faithful Shepherdess*, both in 1886, raised the whole question of natural versus artificial scenery and the juxtaposition of art and reality on which the critics were divided, some preferring natural landscape, others deeming that it spoilt the illusion.

More important was Godwin's staging of Todhunter's *Helena in Troas* at Hengler's Circus also in 1886. By using a circus he anticipated Reinhardt. In it he constructed a Greek stage without any proscenium arch. The actors on a platform were once again in close touch with the audience and not in another world behind a frame. The chorus was in the midst of the spectators who, at last, got some idea of how a Greek play was staged. In the centre of the circle 'which was paved with the semblance of tesselated marble stood the altar of Dionysios and beyond rose the long shallow stage faced with the casts of the temple of Bassae, and bearing the huge portal of the house of Paris and the gleaming battlements of Troy',[130] with the landscape of the Hellespont beyond (Plate 40). For the first time for three centuries an architectural setting with only a slight element of painting was seen in England.

Whilst Godwin was formulating his theory of an integrated production Wagner was promulgating a parallel theory of the Gesamtkunstwerk, in which all artistic elements were to be fused into a whole work of art. This concept was to exercise a potent influence on the new stagecraft. In 1876 he opened his new theatre at Bayreuth which was in amphitheatre form.

129. Godwin, *The Architecture and Costume of Shakespeare's Plays* and *A Few Notes on the Architecture and Costume of the Period of the Play of 'Claudian'*.
130. Oscar Wilde, *Dramatic Review*, May 22, 1886.

PLATE 40. Edward William Godwin, *Helena in Troas* at Hengler's Circus.

Two years later he met Hubert Herkomer, a fashionable portrait painter and amateur musician, who was impressed by Wagner's theories. Herkomer built a little theatre in Bushey where he had his 'pictorial music plays' performed and where he tried out his new ideas. He was in most ways a complete naturalist, made his stage floor uneven so that it was truer to nature, and modelled the cobbles of his street scene. Scenic art was for him an art of illusion which could give a semblance of reality. This reality included mystery and so some part of his picture had to be indistinct and suggestive as it was in nature. He achieved atmospheric effects by a sheet of fine gauze stretched at a slight angle in front of the back-cloth painted with a graduated blue sky; the gauze was played upon with light and cloud effects and, so convinced was the audience that it was seeing the actual sky through an opening

143

at the back, that they had to be shown it was illusion. Her-komer, like Wagner, wanted auditoriums to be in one tier curving upwards from the stage in a fan shape. He proposed a mobile proscenium so that the opening could be made large or small as occasion demanded, but this had already been done by means of sliding panels in the Drury Lane of 1842. He wished to abolish borders, clothes lines in parallel rows, he called them, and footlights, which threw an unnatural light. He saw the possibility of projecting moving clouds by means of a magic lantern. He believed that inexpensive materials, when properly lit, could 'beat the most skilful touch of the painter'. Like Godwin, he strove for a total work of art and he admired Irving for his attempt to create an artistic whole. Though he failed to make the fundamental break with natura-lism he was in many ways a pioneer. His insistence that 'it is through the management of light that we touch the real magic of art' forestalled Appia, and Craig was led to question the established methods after seeing one of his performances and hearing his lecture on 'Scenic Art' in 1894.[131]

The Reforms of Adolphe Appia

Wagner was the catalyst of the revolution in staging that was first brought about by Appia. Like Herkomer, Appia was an admirer both of Wagner's music and his conception of a total work of art; unlike Herkomer, he was disillusioned by the production of the operas at Bayreuth which were in heavy representational style and failed to express Wagner's ele-mental dramas. Appia conceived and designed settings which would be the visual counterpart of Wagner's musical struc-tures and heroic world; music is concerned with time, the scene with space, and these were welded in the actor who used both time and space in his art, so the scene had to be based on

131. For a report of the lecture, see *Magazine of Art*, 1892, pp. 259–264, 316–320. See also Alice Corkran, 'Professor Herkomer's Pictorial Music-Play', *Scottish Art Review*, July 1889, Vol. 2, p. 14; Herkomer, *My School and My Gospel*, 1908.

the movement of actors. Music is abstract and cannot be expressed by a naturalistic setting but only by contrasting masses and forms given movement by the play of light. In 1891–1892 Appia worked out a prompt book for *The Ring* and designed settings for as *Das Rheingold* and *Die Walküre*. He propounded his theories in *La Mise en Scène du Drame Wagnérien*, 1895, and *La Musique et la mise en scène*, 1899, and accompanied these by projected settings which threw realism overboard and were founded on an entirely new conception of scenic art as a symbol in space of the spiritual life. Beginning with the actor, he arranged a central open area which would liberate his movement from walls and back-cloths; the three-dimensional actor was matched by three-dimensional forms and plasticity replaced painting. Since he believed that lighting was primarily for the actor, not for the scene, he reformed it by getting rid of fixed foot and border lights and substituting movable illumination above, which would mould the gestures and groupings of the actors. Colour was also projected by lighting, which here took the place of painting. Costumes were simplified to accord with the setting and all elements combined to express the essential rather than the superficial. Appia did not seek to illustrate the opera but to intensify its mood and emotion. The new function of lighting was assisted by Mariano Fortuny's invention of a new type of indirect illumination and this Appia tried out in a private theatre in Paris in 1903 in scenes from *Carmen* and *Manfred*.

In 1911 Appia came under the influence of Dalcroze, a dancer who was preoccupied with the art of rhythm. Spatial rhythm had been exercising Appia too and he had devised experiments with 'Les espaces rhythmiques', abstract constructions of pillars, cubes, ramps and stairways, forerunner of the permanent set. The two built a theatre in Hellerau where they produced Gluck operas based on their theories, which had a profound effect, particularly on German producers. In the 1920s Appia made designs for several plays. For *Lear* his settings of huge blocks and imposing dimensions signified the primitive yet regal atmosphere of the tragedy, and in another design the series of steps on to an open platform gave a sense of space and universality (Plate 41). Appia also used curtains—sometimes bunched to represent tree trunks, at others draped to contrast with the solid elements. At one swoop Appia cleared the clutter of proscenium arch, painted scenery and stage machinery. His vision was of a sculptural stage, completely non-representational. It was a revolution against the long dominant Italian perspective painted scenery.

PLATE 41. Adolphe Appia, *King Lear*. Projected scene.

Though he never produced in London he held an exhibition of his work in 1922. His influence spread throughout Europe, including Russia, where Meyerhold and Taiov were inspired by his spatial conceptions and his lighting, whilst here his principles were applied by Ricketts in his early work.

The Reforms of Edward Gordon Craig

Gordon Craig and Appia had two fundamental ideas in common; one was the substitution of an abstract, symbolic mounting for one of realistic illustration; the second was the unification of the arts of the theatre. In practice they both emphasised the importance of light as a replacement of painting, though Appia used it for his actors and Craig for his scenes; in many respects they differed in their approaches, but each in his own way revolutionised stage mounting in the name of the art of the theatre. Whereas Appia had insisted on spatial abstraction from the beginning, Craig came to it by degrees; he was to carry it in the end even further than Appia and was to insist on the complete autonomy of the artist director, who would design the setting and costumes, control the lighting and train the actors in movement.

To some extent he too was influenced by music and his first production was of Purcell's *Dido and Aeneas* in 1900[132]. He borrowed from Herkomer's theatre the device of a grey gauze placed in front of a back-cloth and lit from a bridge above the proscenium as well as from the sides to give a depth of colour. He equipped his lights with blue, amber and green gelatines, which he played on the back-cloths, one ultramarine and one grey to express, the change of mood in the opera. In Act I he set up a trellis covered on three sides with leaves and grapes and a small cut cloth was lowered in Act II to give the impression of wreckage. In the last scene the stage, which was stepped behind, was left bare and darkened as the light was taken off the gauze; and after Dido's death a rain of pink rose petals in a shaft of light fell on her until she was blotted

132. I owe much to Edward Craig's book for these descriptions.

out and only the arms of the chorus waving farewell were visible. This immediately showed Craig's imaginative qualities; though as yet his conception was not plastic or three-dimensional but still painted, lighting played a fundamental role. It was an amalgam of old and new but was praised for its simplicity, freedom from distracting detail and use of light and shade. In *The Masque of Love*, Coronet, 1901, set to Purcell's music, painting had been abolished and the setting was a grey canvas box played on with coloured lights which reinforced and symbolised the movements. *Acis and Galatea*, Great Queen Street Theatre, 1902, used a simple back-cloth graduating from white at the bottom through pink to indigo whilst lengths of webbing hung from behind the proscenium, which opened and closed as figures came and went, giving a shadowy appearance. The lovers were on a central mound but everything was unreal and suggestive, leading out the imagination with a harmony of form, colour and motion (Plate 42). Simple materials and simple means marked the production of Housman's *Bethlehem*, Imperial Institute, 1902: a hurdle, sheep made out of sacks, and stars of crystals hung from different heights constituted the décor. Ellen Terry appeared in Ibsen's *The Vikings*, Imperial Theatre, 1903, in which Craig used a rugged rocky slope to which the lighting gave a forbidding aspect. The barbaric nature of the feast was made manifest by rough benches and tables, a central fire, and a platform for the high seat and the spaciousness of the hall was realised in a 'real unreality'. The lovely hues of the light were those of a painter.

Craig discovered Serlio's work and this influenced his production of *Much Ado*. Five Tuscan columns could be moved into different positions at will and were linked with different curtains for a house, balustrades or formal garden, thus forming a set scene. For the church scene he, like Appia, gathered two curtains together in the semblance of columns and behind built up a flight of steps to a platform on which was placed an altar with huge candlesticks and above a partly

PLATE 42. Gordon Craig, *Acis and Galatea*, 1902.

shadowed crucifix; coloured light was thrown from an imaginary stained glass window and into this pool of light the characters entered and from it made their exit. This was Craig's last production in England. Tree, all honour to him, invited him to mount *Macbeth* but was finally dissuaded by Harker after the designs had been prepared. Craig continued to experiment ceaselessly with drawings and models to find his ideal stage. Duse commissioned him to design scenery for *Rosmersholm* at the Pergola Theatre in Florence and he success- fully suggested a place of tragic action by means of an arch, curtains and a huge back window, far removed from the cluttered, stuffy room of realist mounting. In these designs Craig was starting to use the great vertical lines which were to become the hallmark of his settings, so different from Appia's more horizontal built up masses.

As Appia had been, Craig was influenced by the dance, particularly by the free interpretations of Isadora Duncan, and movement became a preoccupation. It was Isadora who proposed to Stanislavski that he invite Craig to Moscow. The play Craig chose was *Hamlet* and for this he devised something entirely new. He made a model of screens which could be moved on the stage to advance or recede, fold or unfold in a series of movements which provided varying compositions in space (Plate 43): 'The scene,' Craig explained, 'remains always the same though incessantly changing'. When enlarged from the model on to canvas-covered wooden frames the screens did not prove altogether practicable as they were apt to fall and so their mobility was reduced to a minimum. For the first court scene Craig devised a striking symbolic effect in which a golden throne was encased in golden walls and the King's enormous golden cloak covered the stage, through cuts in which were seen the backs of the sycophantic courtiers. A model of the screens was given by Craig to W. B. Yeats, who made from it scenes for *The Hour Glass* (Plate 44) at the Abbey Theatre, 1910. Yeats said 'henceforth I shall be able, by means so simple that one laughs, to lay the events of my

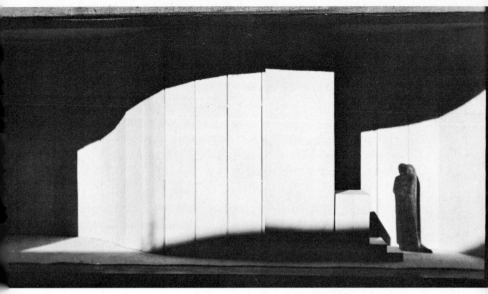

PLATE 43. Gordon Craig, *Hamlet*. Moscow Art Theatre Production.

PLATE 44. Gordon Craig, Yeates's *Hour Glass* with Craig screens.
Abbey Theatre, Dublin.

plays amid a grandeur like that of Babylon; and where there is neither complexity nor compromise nothing need go wrong, no lamps become suddenly unmasked, no ill-painted corner come suddenly into sight . . . he has banished a whole world that wearied me and was undignified and given me forms and lights upon which I can play as upon some stringed instrument'.[133] The screens were an ideal setting for Yeats's symbolic plays. 'The thousand scenes in one scene', as Craig called them, were described in the text and illustrated by engravings in *Scene* and here he expounded his theory of the dramatic role of these mobile screens: 'The scene supplies the simplest form made up of right angles and flat walls and the light runs in and out and all over them'. He used a set of five, with single or double leaf, with ten lamps, and coloured them or the actor by painting in light. Craig had arrived at completely abstract and symbolic designs. In *The Art of the Theatre*, 1911, he gave the world his vision of an ideal theatrical art form. By trying to create a specifically theatric art he went further than Appia. Appia aimed to increase the plasticity of the actor by surrounding him with plastic forms; Craig wished to dispense with the unpredictable actor and replace him by the symbolic 'über-marionette', though he later stated that he did not refer to an actual puppet. He was almost ready to dispense with the play as well and convey the action by scenery, dance, movement and light. He pared everything down to essentials, proposing to stage *Macbeth* in two colours, 'one for the rock, the man' in variations of brown, 'one for the mist, the spirit' in grey. He replaced the idea of the natural by that of the necessary. The old system, used from De Loutherbourg to Harker, must be got rid of for art had nothing to do with realism. In one sentence he came to the heart of the matter: 'the Art of the Theatre is neither acting nor the play; it is not scene or dance; but it consists of all the elements of which these things are composed: action, which is the very spirit of acting; words, which are the body of the

133. *Plays for an Irish Theatre*, 1911.

play; line and colour, which are the very heart of the scene; rhythm, which is the very essence of dance'. This book, his periodical *The Mask* and his school in Florence spread his gospel throughout Europe. Few sought to employ him on account of his unyielding demands, but in 1926 he designed *The Pretenders* for the Royal Copenhagen State Theatre. He used projections for backgrounds and did not scorn mechanical aid for the snow storm. The great flight of steps across the stage was effective for crowd scenes and has often been imitated.

Craig's designs fall into four groups: (1) a simplified scene with some representational elements; (2) curtains; (3) architectural vertical masses; (4) screens. When his ideas percolated on to our stage it was in modified form, as is the British way. Designers are still exploring his possibilities. Thus only recently have we used the moving screens, now electronically controlled and so easy to manipulate. Craig was a genius of high imaginative gifts who, along with Inigo Jones and, to a lesser extent, De Loutherbourg, effected a radical change in scenic convention. He freed the theatre's creative potentialities from the outworn bonds of realism.

William Poel and the Elizabethan Revival

The revival of interest in the Elizabethan theatre with its open stage and minimal scenery was as great an influence on the new stagecraft in England as the work of Appia and Craig, and it was a particularly British contribution to the overthrow of realism. The movement towards staging Shakespeare in a way approximating to the conditions for which his plays were written began in Germany, with Goethe who designed an adaptable and simple setting for *A Midsummer Night's Dream* at Weimar, and Tieck who staged four plays, 1821–1851, on a kind of Elizabethan stage with a permanent setting.

Planché, who may have known Tieck's productions, persuaded Benjamin Webster to allow him to put on *The Taming of the Shrew* at the Haymarket, 1844, with a restored

153

text in a semi-permanent setting consisting of screens and curtains in Renaissance style (Plate 45). The curtains were changed for the transition from inn to hall, the place of action being designated by a placard. The *Times* commented

PLATE 45. J. R. Planché and George Morris, *Taming of the Shrew*. Webster production.

that it gave freedom to the players and closeness to the action but the experiment was not followed up until half a century later.[134]

It was Poel's mission to return Shakespeare to the stage for which he wrote and so reveal the fluidity and dramatic viability of his stagecraft on a bare platform stage without proscenium. He started to put his ideas into practice in 1881 before the experiments of Godwin and Herkomer and in the era of the naturalistic settings of Irving and Tree. Poel's stage was, like the Elizabethan, architectural and not pictorial and he was uncompromising in discarding scenery. The first quarto *Hamlet*, St. George's Hall, 1881, was produced on an empty draped platform, the first such presentation in Europe. All he required was an inner recess, two doors and a platform of the size of the Fortune. 'I wanted,' he said, 'to show that there was a possible movement on the Elizabethan stage not possible on the proscenium stage'. In 1893 he converted the Royalty Theatre into as close a resemblance to the Fortune as possible, though he was saddled with the proscenium. He put on *Measure for Measure* in Elizabethan costume and proved that scenic accessories were unnecessary and, indeed, a hindrance (Plate 46). Poel was happier with the open stages of halls. He gave *Twelfth Night* in two halls in 1895, *The Comedy of Errors* in Gray's Inn the same year and *Twelfth Night* again in the Middle Temple Hall in 1897, arranged according to the recently discovered drawing of the Swan Theatre. He met with opposition from some critics, notably William Archer, but support from others who did not miss the absence of scenery. Shaw even opined that the platform stage was suitable for any play. He introduced a bold experiment in *The Comedy of Errors* when a procession passed through the midst of the audience, thus preceding Reinhardt's similar attempt to link spectators and stage.

134. Jan McDonald, '*The Taming of the Shrew* at the Haymarket Theatre, 1844 and 1847', *Nineteenth Century British Theatre*, ed. K. Richards and P. Thomson, 1971.

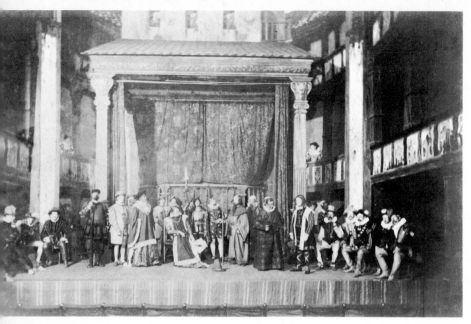

PLATE 46. William Poel, *Measure for Measure*.

Tree, who was not averse to new ideas, invited Poel to stage *The Two Gentlemen of Verona* at one of his famous Shakespeare Festivals in 1910 and had an apron stage built over the orchestra pit, as has been frequently done in our own day. Tree was sufficiently impressed to retain it and the lighting from the balcony for his own *Henry VIII*.

One of Poel's most famous productions was of *Everyman* in 1901. In this case the recess was decorated with trees and mountains in Bellini style. Reinhardt saw it and there is little doubt that it was the inspiration of his famous production of *Jedermann* at Salzburg.

Poel tried to produce the soft effect of candlelight, but at Stratford in 1913 he contrasted a warm glow with cold limelight. His costumes were Elizabethan even for *Troilus*, where the opposing Trojans were dressed in masque habits.

By the end of his career in 1931 Poel had proved his case and had inaugurated the movement towards an open stage.

Producers such as Granville Barker, Barry Jackson, Harcourt Williams, Iden Payne and Robert Atkins were deeply indebted to him, though they were not so uncompromising. Productions at Stratford and the Old Vic strove for the speed and elasticity which he had achieved, and our modern open stages in Stratford, Ontario, and Chichester proclaim the validity of his ideas. The earliest attempt to build a small theatre in Elizabethan terms was made by Poel's disciple, Nugent Monck, at the Maddermarket in Norwich.[135] Monck was less austere than Poel and used on occasion painted back curtains to set the play's location and to introduce more colour. From 1921 onwards he produced the whole Shakespeare canon and demonstrated how much all gained by the fluidity of the stage (Plate 47).

Poel released the imagination of an audience clogged with superfluous illustration. Unlike Appia and Craig, he did not create a replacement but reverted to the simple staging of the Elizabethan tradition.

Granville Barker's Stylised Productions

The simplified staging of Shakespeare initiated by Poel was popularised by Barker in less academic reconstructions. Barker was also influenced by Craig and by German producers who, some years before, had produced Shakespeare in permanent settings. Barker's season at the Savoy, 1912–1914, aroused passionate controversy but pointed the way to the staging of Shakespeare in the future. The new stagecraft was filtered through him to become the stylised productions of the period between the wars.

Barker made what approximation he could in a west-end theatre to an Elizabethan lay-out. He built out a forestage over the orchestra, reduced the acting area of the stage by a false proscenium, and raised it by two steps; it thus served as an enlarged version of the Elizabethan inner stage and was the portion for which scenery was provided. Proscenium doors

135. See Charles Rigby, *Maddermarket Mondays*, 1933.

PLATE 47. *Taming of the Shrew*. Maddermarket Theatre.

were installed, footlights were abolished and the forestage was lit by spots from the dress circle.[136]

Barker followed Craig in believing in the supervision by one man of all facets of staging but, as he was not himself a designer, he employed artists of the calibre of Norman Wilkinson, Albert Rutherston and Charles Ricketts to carry out, in conjunction with the producer, the whole visual side of the presentation. In order to play as full a text as possible he needed flexible scenery, and his three Shakespeare productions followed a pattern of two permanent scenes occupying

136. M. St. Clare Byrne, 'Fifty Years of Shakespearean Production', *Shakespeare Survey*, 1949, Vol. 2, pp. 7–10; *Stage Year Book*, 1914, pp. 19–20.

the whole stage and decorative curtains which could be drawn or closed. There was a frank acknowledgement of scenic illusion as opposed to reality, so that the curtains were hung in folds even when decorated with stylised woods or landscapes. No attempt was made at more than a suggestion of time or place; the decoration was based only on the spirit of the play. Form and colour were carefully thought out and carried through in scenery, costume and lighting.

The first production was *The Winter's Tale*, with décor by Wilkinson and costumes by Rutherston, in which the palace scene was a harmony of white pilasters and gold curtains. Wilkinson devised two scenes for *Twelfth Night*, a formal garden with artificial triangular trees and a gate and walls.

The production that roused most controversy was *A Midsummer Night's Dream*, famous for its golden fairies in orientalised costumes. Theseus's palace consisted of columns with steps to a stage where the mechanicals performed before courtiers lounging on couches; behind was a star flecked cloth. Wilkinson's wood scene was painted in dyes in a pattern on the curtains of green, blue and purple, which were changed by lighting (Plate 48). The ground was covered with a green carpet flecked by flowers. The garland and gauze canopy were lit by flickering fire flies and glow worms. These suggestions were sufficient to convey the spirit of the play; elaboration was reserved for the costumes.

Rutherston was the decorator (Barker preferred the term) for *Androcles and the Lion* and *Le Mariage Forcé* at Barker's season at the St. James in 1913. For the former he used a front curtain and a revolving scene in three dimensions, which was denounced by one critic as 'a sea-green Futurist cave'. His working model for the Molière comedy (Plate 49) is an early example of a permanent set with four doors, whose formality is admirably in keeping with the spirit of the play.

In a lecture on 'Decoration in the Art of the Theatre' given in 1912[137] Rutherston set out his ideas for the perfection of

137. *Monthly Chapbook*, August 1919, Vol. 1, No. 2.

PLATE 48. Norman Wilkinson, *A Midsummer Night's Dream*. Granville-Barker production.

the whole. The decorator must be in control not only of every detail of the decoration but of lighting and grouping, in association with the producer: 'To design alone is useless, to carry out the designs and to know exactly how they should and can be carried out, is one of the most important things of all. . . . A designer must be architect and mathematician, painter, sculptor, carpenter and dressmaker'. What was needed was not any form of exact realism but 'creation, imagination, vision'. Little thought had been given in England, as Appia had given it, to the relationship between the living, moving actor and his background. Rutherston worked out his spatial relationships on a scale model and then experimented with

PLATE 49. Albert Rutherston, *Le Mariage Forcé*. Granville-Barker production.

lighting. Form and proportion came first, then colour and decoration. The art, the charm of the theatre was its artificiality. The influence of Craig, for whom Rutherston had a great admiration, is paramount in these views.

Charles Ricketts

Ricketts's work for the theatre covered the period from 1906 to 1931, during which he was involved in scenery and costumes for over fifty productions. Appia rather than Craig was the major influence on his work. Ricketts too recognised that Wagner had been the moving spirit in reforming the stage, admired his theatre at Bayreuth, where the whole audience had an equal chance to see and hear, but was also horrified at the realistic scenery he accepted for his operas. Appia's

161

rejection of realism, and his stagecraft of abstract masses and ever changing light, appealed to Ricketts, but he was not convinced that this form of staging was suitable for every play. He questioned whether the moods of lyric and poetic dramas, to which he was particularly drawn, could be subjected to a few principles. Each play, he believed, should be decorated according to its mood and he carried out décors in many diverse styles. A play such as *Samson Agonistes* required only a wall or curtain with entrances. For *Pélleas and Mélisande* it would be sufficient to use circular curtains to suggest colonnades with vistas, labyrinths, the stalactite caves, the gloom of forests. Ricketts agreed with Appia that the stage floor should be broken into different levels to enhance significant movement: 'a staircase alone may suggest more of the majesty of a building than an entire palace'. He believed that what was needed was a comfortable auditorium, a much deeper stage and a reform of lighting, which was twenty years behind the times.[138]

Barker employed Ricketts for his productions of Maeterlinck's plays and as costume designer for Shaw's early comedies. The symbolic plays were well suited to Ricketts's talents. Symbolism, which stemmed from France and the work of Paul Fort at the Théâtre d'Art in Paris in 1890, had not caught on in England, though it deeply influenced the work of Yeats, for whose *King's Threshold* Ricketts designed scenery. Both Fort and Lugné-Poë had produced several of Maeterlinck's plays, whilst Meyerhold in Russia had mounted three of them with symbolic colours on screens. Ricketts chose another way with *The Betrothal*, 1921, creating a series of stage pictures which reflected the play's mingling of simple life and the fantastic, and forming a unity of scale and colour.

Ricketts also used symbolic key colouring—as, for instance, blue for Wilde's *Salomé*, green for Barker's *A Miracle* and red for the barabaric theme of Binyon's *Attila*.

Ricketts made his name with *King Lear*, Herbert Trench's

138. 'The Art of Stage Decoration', *Pages in Art*, 1913, pp. 229–247.

PLATE 50. Charles Ricketts, *King Lear*.

opening production at the Haymarket in 1909. For this he used grey tones and suggestions of massive architecture (Plate 50) with a proscenium which as Herkomer had proposed, contracted or expanded to give contrasting effects of height and breadth. Ricketts would have preferred a bare stage as background as 'more barbaric and remote than the canvas cromlechs of the actual production'.[139] Yet the great monolithic forms express the feeling of the tragedy more than any painted scene.

Ricketts's later work contained more realistic elements. For *Saint Joan*, 1924, he took the kitchen at Chilham Castle where he lived as a model for the first scene, his stained glass

139. Ricketts, letter to Huntly Carter, 1910. Victoria and Albert Museum.

163

from King's College Chapel, and himself designed the Gothic tapestries. The effect was very far from archaeological and the scenery was thought of not as a reproduction of the past but as an evocation of it.

As an artist much influenced by Japanese art, Ricketts was a natural choice for the remounting of *The Mikado*, Princes, 1926. He dressed it in early 18th century Japanese court style, but in restrained colours. He gave dignity and artistry to the production, but was criticised for being too heavy-handed for the light tone of the operetta. The same rebuke was levelled against his resettings of *The Gondoliers*, Savoy, 1929, in 'stiff and solemn splendour',[140] though his green and gold throne room with paintings in the style of Veronese was a perfect décor for the Venetian fashions of the Goldoni period.

If he seems to have slipped back into an ornate realism it must be remembered that he was an admirer of Bakst as well as Appia and that he held that the theatre had many valid styles.

Reinhardt in England

The German theatre had absorbed the ideas of Appia and Craig before they began to take effect in England. It was also making use of the new inventions of the revolving stage and the developed types of cyclorama. The former, invented by Lauterschläger in 1896, made it possible to present five or more scenes and thus avoid shifting or waits. But the scenes had to be fitted into the segments of a circle. The new type of cyclorama was of two kinds—the 'rund horizont', a backing stretched on vertical rollers, and the 'dome horizont', which partially covered the stage and so prevented awkward edges being visible. Here the flat version with curved ends was generally adopted. The cyclorama acted as a light reflector. Fortuny had invented an arc lamp which replaced the incandescent variety and this enabled light to be diffused rather than direct. Bands of coloured silk, on De Louther-

164   140. *Times*, October 22, 1929.

bourg's principle, which travelled on rollers, reflected light in desired tints and this gave a more luminous and soft effect on the neutral cyclorama than direct light on a painted back-cloth. Both colour and white were rendered in purer forms.

Max Reinhardt has been called 'the Great Eclectic' because he carried out his belief that every play must be mounted in a fashion that would suit it alone. He did not have one style of presentation but a different style for each presenta-tion. He was influenced by Craig's curtain scenery and his contrasts of light and shade, and he came nearest of all his contemporaries to that amalgam of the artist and practical man which Craig had envisaged. He was an organiser who could unify ideas he had absorbed from many sources.

The productions of Craig and Poel had been seen only by limited audiences when Reinhardt brought the mime play, *Sumurûn*, to the Coliseum in 1911. The theatre had a revolving stage which had been installed in 1904, and for his seven tableaux Reinhardt used it so that the main feature of one section served as a subsidiary for the next, thus avoiding the segmental wedge. The story was set in the East but Ernst Stern, the scene designer, obtained his effects not by the sumptuous mounting of *Sardanapalus* but by simple settings with harmonious colour contrasts. The backgrounds were white, against which were set the colours of rugs, the bright wares of a merchant's shop and the effective silhouette of the towers and minarets of the palace against the deep night sky. Each scene had a dominant colour, a feature we have seen used by Ricketts. For the prologue Reinhardt had a Japanese 'flower path' constructed, down which the actor walked through the audience. *Sumurûn* was a sensation and was influential in establishing here a simplified setting and an atmospheric unity.[141]

C. B. Cochran saw Reinhardt's production of *Oedipus Rex* in the Schumann Circus in Berlin where, like Godwin before

141. Felix Felton, 'Max Reinhardt in England', *Theatre Research*, 1962, Vol. 5, p. 3.

him, he brought the action into the midst of the audience, and immediately engaged him for a London production. This was *The Miracle*, 1911, given in the vast arena of Olympia with Stern as designer. Here Reinhardt carried out his dream of incorporating play and audience into one setting. Stern converted Olympia into the semblance of a cathedral in which the audience sat to witness the mimed play (Plate 51). This was achieved both by built scenery and massed shadows. Like the Meiningers, Reinhardt employed leaders to organise his crowd scenes and he included a number of processions. The new spot lighting technique enabled him to pick out individuals or model groups. The result was impressive and gave the large audience a sense of actually participating in the experience, a forerunner of the different type of audience participation popular today. Ricketts admired the vast scale, unlike anything yet seen in England, and the whole organisation but hated the Gothic Olympia 'designed by the German Emperor in disguise'.[142]

In 1912 Reinhardt staged *Oedipus Rex* at the Lyceum with scenery by Stern and Alfred Roller. The Mycenean or Cretan setting was denounced by Gilbert Murray as merely savage. The scheme was black and white against a deep blue sky but the dazzling white of the palace was occasionally relieved by touches of colour. The entrance of the blinded Oedipus through the auditorium caused a sensation.

In 1932 Cochran again brought Reinhardt over to stage Offenbach's *Helen* with rococo and Empire scenery and costumes by Oliver Messel. On a revolving stage Messel designed three scenes for the three acts. Steeped in period atmosphere, he created an elaborate pastiche in which 17th century perspective principles were used in a kind of mocking fantasy. Wit had entered scene design. Messel also experimented with new materials such as cellophane, American cloth and gauze covered with gelatine to give a varnished appearance. It was a stylised, decorative setting of a kind that

142. *Self Portrait*, ed. Cecil Lewis, 1939, p. 172.

Within the image, the following labels are visible:

LIMELIGHTS
WORKED FROM
3 GALLERIES
SUSPENDED
FROM THE ROOF

ENTRANCE
& EXIT

ORCHESTRA

ENTRANCE
FOR PERFORMERS

AT
BOTH
DOORS
SHOWN
IN

EXIT

SECTION TAKEN
OUT OF FLOORING TO
SHOW THE UNDERGROUND
ARRANGEMENTS TO RAISE AND
LOWER STAGE

POSITION OF
HILL AND TREES
WHEN IN THE
ARENA

RAILS ON WHICH
THE HILL AND
TREES MOVES INTO
THE ARENA

LESSER
SLIDING-DOOR
WHICH FITS
INTO THE
GREAT
DOOR

GREAT SLIDING
DOOR

PLAYERS
MAKING
READY
IN THE
CORRIDORS

PLATE 51. Ernst Stern, *The Miracle*. Reinhardt production at Olympia.

was characteristic of scenery between the wars.

Reinhardt never used an abstract setting, but he adapted the new stagecraft to his spectacles. He was willing to employ any technique that suited a play, but did not exploit machinery or tehnical devices for their own sake. Because he was a brilliant middle-of-the-road man, he had a good deal more influence on contemporary staging than the extremists.

Diaghilev's Russian Ballet

The coronation year 1911 was an *annus mirabilis* for influential

167

stage settings from abroad. It saw not only *Sumurûn* but the first visit of Diaghilev's ballet at Covent Garden. Diaghilev and his artists represented the renaissance in Russian art in revolt against the dead hand of naturalism. Little or nothing had been known of Russian art in the theatre and the impact was astounding. The ballets were a unity in which movement, music and décor were fused into an overall harmony. Artistically, it was, however, a painter's and not a plastic décor and at first represented a revival of romance in the theatre.

The artistic director, Alexandre Benois, who designed scenery and costumes and invented the theme of *Pavillon d'Armide*, reverted to baroque spectacle, and in 1914 exploited his vibrant blues in *Le Rossignol*. His setting for *Petrouchka*, 1912, mingled Russian folk elements with glimpses of orientalism. Roerich and Anisfield expressed the barbaric wildness of tribal wars and the vast spaces of the steppes in the low, luridly lit setting for the *Prince Igor* dances, and Roerich continued his exploration of the primitive with his scenery for *Le Sacre du Printemps* in 1913. But it was Bakst who created the greatest sensation with his voluptuous *Schéhérazade* (Plate 52). Nothing like the clashing juxtaposed colours of orange and pink, contrasted with blue and green, had been seen on the English stage. His bold massed colours and great hanging draperies invoked a gorgeous sensuality far removed from Stern's white settings and simplified forms. It was an incarnation of the ballet's mood and theme. Bakst was many sided and also created the tender atmosphere of the virginal, moonlit room in *Spectre de la Rose*, the unreal orange and yellow trees as a backround for the dancers' frieze in *L'Après Midi d'un Faune* and the ultramarine setting of *Carnaval*. The inward sloping walls of *Thamar* expressed both the Caucasian background and the menacing doom of the legend.

When Diaghilev returned to London after the war he had become associated with the painters of the avant-garde of the School of Paris and he introduced their stage work. Picasso designed the bold and simple scene for *Le Tricorne* in 1919,

PLATE 52. Léon Bakst, *Schehérézade.*

which recreated the heat of Spain, and the drop curtain for *Parade*; Derain the drop for *La Boutique Fantasque,* and Braque introduced cubism into the English theatre in *Les Fâcheux* and *Zephyr and Flora* in 1925. In the same year Marie Laurencin showed her witty, post-impressionist setting for *Les Biches.* In 1927 it was the turn of constructivism in *La Chatte,* where the scenery by Gabo and Pevsner was of talc which dazzled with reflected light. However, Yakalov's constructions of a machine with wheels and pulleys for *Le Pas d'Acier* went too far and failed to draw. The ballet had provided an education in the schools of modern art and prepared the way for modern design.

Then in 1921 Diaghilev once more astonished London with the most sumptuous production of a classical ballet, *The* 169

Sleeping Princess. Bakst's settings were his masterpiece, in which he absorbed and even imitated the work of the Bibienas.[143] The Princess went to sleep in the baroque and awoke in the rococo. Bakst had studied the designs and costumes of both periods and Berain and Boquet were rifled for ideas. He employed the diagonal perspective in a magnificent flight of steps with further perspectives seen through the cut columns, and Negro guards painted on the canvas. By contrast, the rococo scene was light and open with characteristic Salomonic columns. This wonderful creation was the last of the baroque glories, but it was a failure, and left Diaghilev bankrupt. Bakst died in 1924, leaving as legacy his use of intense, vibrant colour and, as with Benois, a capacity to distil the quintessence of a period or place. His influence ensured that period scene painting continued in the work of his successors, who are considered in the next chapter.

Diaghilev returned the painter to the theatre and demonstrated how new art styles could be absorbed into it. Our painted scenery today owes much to his flair, his restless innovation, and his employment of great artists.

143. Deborah Howard, 'A Sumptuous Revival', *Apollo*, April 1970, pp. 301–307.

CHAPTER IX

The Last Half Century

Expressionism and Constructivism

Two new types of setting emerged after the first world war—expressionism from defeated Germany and constructivism from revolutionary Russia. The former illustrated plays which saw men as cyphers in the grip of big business and machines; the latter extolled workers and machines as hopes for the future. Though both were concerned with the dominance of the machine, they were ideologically at opposite ends of the pole. Expressionism was subjective and tormented and the plays moved through a succession of swiftly changing scenes. The décor was distorted and nightmarish, often symbolising the subjective agony of the protagonist. Out of focus optics and curious angles expressed more than a touch of dementia. New techniques were inspanned to create these effects which, in their shifting variety, had been influenced by the cinema. Scenes were projected and dissolved into one another like dreams; revolving stages, wagons and elevators secured the rapid changes; apron stages brought the horror nearer to the spectators. Jessner and his designers, Pirchan and Klein, were the principal scenographers of the movement in Germany. It was, however, the film of *Dr. Caligari's Cabinet* which disseminated the type of décor throughout Europe. In England, though some expressionist plays were produced, the style never took root. Paul Shelving's scenery for Kaiser's *Gas*, Birmingham Repertory Theatre, 1923 (Plate 53), is a Cubist version of the deforming spirit. Later the distortions were used in unsuitable plays, such as *The Merchant of Venice* at Stratford, where crazy houses and bridges were reduced by Komisarjev-

PLATE 53. Paul Shelving, *Gas*. Model for Birmingham Repertory
Company.

sky to a mere style inexpressive of the character of the drama.

Contructivism confined scenery to strictly functional purposes and was in itself a glorification of the machine. The
settings consisted of levels, scaffolding, ramps and ladders on
which actors performed acrobatic feats sometimes, as in
Popova's setting for *The Magnanimous Cuckold* for Meyerhold,
172   accompanied by constantly rotating machinery. Aesthetic

effect was scorned; dynamic and kinetic elements were paramount. Tairov was the producer mainly associated with the
style and his production of Chesterton's *Man Who Was
Thursday*, 1923–1924, was constructed on several storeys
linked by lifts and stairways and made use of screens and
projected titles. These scaffoldings were a type of anti-art
contrived for the antics of the actors. This style, first brought
here by Diaghilev, showed designers the advantages of multi-
level settings and was the forerunner of skeletal erections easy
to construct and shift. Thus Doria Paston's mounting for *The
Government Inspector*, Cambridge Festival Theatre, 1932 (Plate
54), was influenced by constructivism, though without complicated levels. Sophie Fedorovitch also used scaffolds, but
neither expressed through them the dominance of the machine.

PLATE 54. Doria Paston, *Government Inspector*. Cambridge Festival
Theatre.

In our own day Sean Kenny has come nearest to the original bare forms. Both expressionism and constructivism were seen here in watered down versions, which, while supplying designers with new types of mounting, had lost their original purpose and impetus.

Revue

During and after the first world war the most advanced scenery was shown in revue. Owing to the intimate revue's character of swiftly changing sketches and the shortage of materials, decorators were compelled to use their ingenuity. They popularised the curtained stage within a false proscenium and used decorative devices in which movement, colour and lighting coalesced to express the background of a topical skit. Charlot's revues in particular had a witty chic and artistry and conveyed a sense of intimacy from the use of a false proscenium and simple, decorated cloths and curtains; sometimes the bare walls of the theatre formed part of the setting, as so often today. A neo-primitive style of childlike distortion and colouring also emerged, as in the seaside scene for Cochran's wartime revue, *More*. It had probably derived from Gontcharova's setting for Diaghilev's *Coq d'Or*, 1914, with its Russian fairy tale atmosphere, and was popularised in 1921 and after by the visits of Balieff's *Chauve Souris* with its toylike miniature scenes. On a more lavish scale, C. B. Cochran's post-war revues were designed by scenographers who had absorbed many of the pre-war experiments and who were influenced by the Russian Ballet and the Moscow Arts Theatre. Such, for example, was *The League of Notions* in 1921 which, in addition to the Russian influences, included a scene with masks by Benda. These shows conditioned audiences into accepting stylisation. In a series of annual revues from 1926 Cochran employed Oliver Messel, who provided him with the lavish picturesqueness he required, but whose sense of design and colour, touch of fantasy and period expertise ensured a high artistic quality. Like Diaghilev, Cochran employed modern artists, among them Christopher Wood, Christian Bérard, Rex Whistler and Doris Zinkeisen, all noted for their feeling for period and place.

The art nouveau movement was introduced on the stage by Erté in his work for revue, notably *It's in the Bag*, Saville, 1937, with its Aztec ballet. His sinuous, sensuous lines, his outsize trains and head-dresses, and his use of lavishly gowned or partially nude actresses as part of the décor were voluptuous, elegant, fantastic and slightly decadent.

Permanent Sets

The period between the wars was one of consolidation and digestion of the new theories which had made the first two decades of the century so exciting. The advances were technological rather than aesthetic. Scene designers exploited the curtains and permanent sets which had been introduced by Wilkinson, Rutherston and Ricketts.

When Lovat Fraser mounted *As You Like It* at Stratford in 1919[144] the setting was denounced as futuristic, though decorative scenery of the kind had been established before the war and he had taken his cue from illuminated manuscripts. He followed Barker's designers in limiting himself to two scenes, the court and the forest, and indicating changes of locality by simple additions. Fraser had a fine colour sense and preferred to dye his materials to secure the exact tint he needed. The backgrounds were of broad tones of blue and green, against which he set orange and vermilion costumes. There were no distracting details and so attention was not filched from the play.

Fraser's most famous design was for *The Beggar's Opera* under Nigel Playfair at the Lyric Hammersmith in 1920. A

---

144. E.O.H. 'Mr. C. Lovat Fraser's Designs for "As You Like It" ', *Studio*, 1919, Vol. 7, p. 63; T. C. Kemp and J. C. Trewin, *The Stratford Festival*, 1953.

PLATE 55. Claude Lovat Fraser, *The Beggar's Opera*. Nigel Playfair
production.

tight economy forced him to stage it in one permanent set
(Plate 55), which he varied by means of curtains to represent
indoor and outdoor localities. With his fine period sense he
created the feeling of the 18th century with minimal scenery
and carefully designed costumes. He sought out what he
believed was the basic shape of a period and designed the
scenes as if he were living in them. *The Beggar's Opera* made
the permanent set popular and fashionable, and it was an
obvious boon to the hard-pressed repertory theatres.

For Karsavina's ballets at the Coliseum, Fraser worked
with enclosing curtains, as in the emerald ones with toylike
patterns and a built up arch mounted on wheels for *Nursery*

176

PLATE 56. George Sheringham, *Twelfth Night*. Stratford-upon-Avon.

Rhymes. In his short life he worked in several styles, but always his artistry, colour sense and care for detail vindicated his non-realistic approach.

George Sheringham, who also worked for Playfair, possessed a subtle sense of period and recaptured the spirit of the 18th century in *The Duenna*, 1924, and *Love in a Village*, 1928, for the latter of which he painted a drop curtain after Rowlandson. He shared with Ricketts in 1928 the remounting of the Gilbert and Sullivan operas. He was one of the team of scene painters engaged by Bridges-Adams at Stratford in 1932 and 1934. He followed Wilkinson's recipe of alternating set scenes and curtains. In *Twelfth Night* set scenes for Olivia's house and garden alternate with curtains, loosely hung and unrealistically crumpled, for a street painted in perspective and for Orsino's palace (Plate 56). He too supplemented painting 177 by dyeing materials and props. Sheringham complained that the commercial theatre failed to employ the three or four designers who had vision and taste sufficient to revive the art of stage decoration. Scenery and costumes, he believed, should be designed by one artist, whereas costumes were often made by a firm without consultation with the designer. He was of the opinion that coloured lighting projection was not enough since it omitted form.[145]

Bridges-Adams, when he became director of the Shakespeare Festivals at Stratford in 1919, installed a cyclorama and, in 1920, used truck stages and traverses for *The Merchant of*

PLATE 57. William Lewis Telbin, *Much Ado about Nothing*. Church scene. Alexander production.

145. *Design in the Theatre.*

PLATE 58. Walter Bridges-Adams, *Much Ado about Nothing*. Church scene.
Stratford-upon-Avon.

Venice. He also used semi-permanent settings for *Macbeth*,
Richard III and *Much Ado* in 1923. His church scene for the
last, when compared with Telbin's elaborate version for
Alexander of twenty-five years before, is evidence of the
simplicity which had been attained (Plates 57 and 58). Adams
believed that decorative elements must be subordinated to the
drama and the actor, and that it was the business of decorators
to make the audience feel at home with the play quickly and
unobrusively.[146] Bridges-Adams in his last years at Stratford
gathered round him a group of outstanding designers who
specialised in permanent settings, curtains and stylised
decoration. In addition to Sheringham were Wilkinson,

146. E.O.H. 'The Designs of W. Bridges Adams', *Studio*, 1927, Vol. 28,
    p. 156.

Aubrey Hammond and Komisarjevsky. Hammond was scenic supervisor in 1932 and used a rolling stage in *Julius Caesar*. The Forum was built up on lifts but a curtain act drop served for Caesar's house and a back curtain for Lepidus's house, a mingling of new and old. A movable cave in *The Tempest* could be placed in various positions; a permanent set was designed for *Love's Labour's Lost* and an inner proscenium resembling a rood screen for *Henry V*, an example of the various types of setting now available to the designer.

By the time the Shakespeare Memorial Theatre was rebuilt in 1932 Stratford had become a centre for modern designers. The most experimental of these was Theodore Komisarjevsky. We have noted his expressionist style in *The Merchant of Venice*. In 1933 he introduced aluminium scenery which caught the light, an early example of the employment of metal. But it was his *Lear* which made the deepest impression by its single unit set of wide steps which could be placed at different angles for changes of locality (Plate 59). Beautifully graduated lighting played on this bare and spacious stage and silhoutted groups of actors against the sky, giving a sense of universality. Mr. Trewin has described how the short scenes were 'played in pools of light which flowed and swirled in changing colours until the whole setting was embraced for the purposes of crowded court or open heath'. In the battle scenes 'an eerie glare from the beach below and an ever-ascending smoke appeared to be attending men striving with fate on the top of the world'. The light died slowly at the end as 'darkness descended step by step down the stage'.[147]

One of the most effective permanent sets at Stratford was constructed by Tanya Moiseiwitsch for the cycle of history plays in 1951. It consisted of timber platforms and galleries linked by stairways (Plate 60). The central wide gateway suggested an inner stage. This fine set proved an excellent vehicle for speed, continuity and processions, and was even found viable for *Othello*.

180   147. T. C. Kemp and J. C. Trewin, *op. cit.*, p. 179.

PLATE 59. Theodore Komisarjevsky, *King Lear*. Stratford-upon-Avon.

The Birmingham Repertory Theatre under Barry Jackson produced a distinguished and versatile designer in Paul Shelving. He worked in many styles: the symbolist for the mysterious forest in *The Immortal Hour* with its patterned tree trunks and misty atmosphere; modern setting and dress in *Cymbeline* in 1923, one of the first of its kind; curtains and cutouts with a snake theme in *Back to Methuselah*; a medieval multiple scene for *The Interlude of Youth*, and for Gheon's *Marvellous History of Saint Bernard*, in which hell was situated in part of the stalls. Under the influence of Appia and Craig he suggested a forest in *Rashomon* by shapely screens distributed as in a Japanese theatre. His mounting of *The Tempest*, Stratford, 1946, was magical and fantastic with ranges of

PLATE 60. Tanya Moiseiwitsch, *Henry VIII*. Permanent set for Stratford-upon-Avon.

coloured crags. Shelving was a fine colourist who enjoyed blocking out broad masses in patterns. He demonstrated what could be achieved by the new stagecraft on a small budget.

Terence Gray and the Cambridge Festival Theatre

This was the most experimental theatre of its time. Gray produced over a hundred plays between 1926 and 1933 in this converted 18th century playhouse. He drew his ideas from the new movements in Europe; not only from Appia, Craig and Reinhardt, but from Lugné-Poë and Copeau in France, Jessner in Germany and Meyerhold in Russia. Their theory and practice served him for an all-out attack on 'the

182

old game of illusion, glamour and all the rest of the nineteenth century hocus pocus and bamboozli'.[148] He aimed to sweep away 'the cobwebs of external reality', replacing them by pure aestheticism in formal, stylised productions. He eliminated the proscenium and built a thrust stage the width of the building, from which a fan-shaped flight of steps descended into the auditorium. Gangways through the audience led to these steps and provided entrances for the actors. The stage was divided into three sections. Upstage was a 40 foot high cylindrical cyclorama, in front of which the stage was slightly raised and made to roll forward in three divisions, giving access to an entrance understage. In the centre downstage was a revolving stage on which architectural settings were placed; these could then be rotated to show their different aspects—thus emphasising their sculptural, three-dimensional quality. On this instrument variations of form, movement and grouping could be played. This pile of platforms with ramps and flights of steps has been compared to the Mappin Terraces, but proved a flexible set piece which dominated the stage and ensured a continuous flow of action. Four pairs of reversible curtains, two up and two down stage, could be run on tracks to change scenes during the performance. Harold Ridge, Gray's lighting expert, who was a disciple of Appia, installed one of the finest lighting systems in the world, which illuminated settings and costumes with symbolic and shifting colours.

Gray's most original innovation was his hollow box system. It consisted of twenty-four light framework cubes, drums, and cylinders in varying sizes, the cubes being painted pale blue or grey, the cylinders dark grey or terra cotta. They could be built up into innumerable combinations and, when lit with colours, could suggest mountains, forests and other natural forms. They could 'be built into vast towering architectural

148. 'This Age in the Theatre', *Bookman*, October 1932, Vol. 32, p. 11; T. Gray, 'The Festival Theatre in Cambridge', *Theatre Arts Monthly*, September 1926, Vol. 10, pp. 585–586.

PLATE 61. Terence Gray, *Oedipus*. Cambridge Festival Theatre.

forms expressive of the atmosphere of the piece and lit by beams of coloured light playing on them and altering with each passing phase of the action and each varying emotional condition of the actor'.[149] Both boxes and screens, arranged on different levels for each play, were used for *The Oresteia*. Lighting was symbolic, as when a baleful green announced the entrances of Clytemnestra. A combination of boxes and steps used in *Oedipus* served to position actors symbolically: thus Oedipus at the end descended from the flight before the palace entrance and was replaced by Creon (Plate 61). The movement was perpendicular towards the audience rather than horizontal in front of it.

An aluminium ramp, which rose in a steep curve and vanished above, and which took the colours of the changing light, was employed in *Henry VIII*. Actors made their entrances on to the spiral through a blue plush curtain at the rear and the king was placed in an alcove on one side of the curve.[150]

149. Gray, *Dance Drama*, 1926.
150. C. Rigby, *op. cit.*, pp. 103–108.

The costumes were stylised to resemble playing cards, thus affording a further remove from historical reality.

The emotional possibilities of the great screens were illustrated in *The Tremendous Lover*, based on the legend of Deirdre. At first overpowering and sinister, lit by the crimson glow of buring Emain, they modulated to pale blue and moonlight green to express the lovers' mood of peace and serenity. The screens were of varying heights and could be used separately or hinged together, usually in conjunction with three-dimensional elements, a feature in which Gray differed from Craig.

In some productions, such as *Romeo and Juliet*, 1928, and *Hassan*, 1931, medieval-type multiple settings were employed, the lighting picking out each unit as it was required and dimming the rest. Ridge also used front projections on to the cyclorama under the influence of Erwin Piscator's experiments. The struggle with the gorilla in *The Hairy Ape*, for instance, was projected in outsize shadows, intensifying the dramatic effect.

Gray designed many scenes himself but also worked with Doria Paston from 1928 (Plate 54 p. 173) and Hedley Briggs. Like Craig, he believed that the artistic director was the centre of the production to be served both by play and actors. He too was influenced by the dance and by movement, through which he often interpreted the relationships and states of mind of his characters. This interest also proved a great asset in his productions of Greek tragedy.

Some of his experiments were way out and his audience was an intellectual élite. Though his immediate impact was slight, the stage of our day owes much to his combination of architecture and lighting to emphasise essential and significant forms. He was a visionary who became the most avant-garde director of his day in England, which up till then had lagged behind the experimental staging on the Continent.

Two other experimental theatres were the Everyman, run by Norman Macdermott, 1920–1925, succeeded by Malcolm

Morley, and the Gate, run by Peter Godfrey, 1925–1934, succeeded by Norman Marshall. Macdermott was a disciple of Craig, who envisaged his theatre as a 'communal effort to which every artist concerned contributes his talent'. As a scene designer, he used unit sets which could be arranged in different patterns and lit in various ways. Because he considered the technique of the pictorial artist unsuitable to the stage whose material should be plastic, he employed painting sparingly, relying on the emotional quality of light on neutral surfaces.[151] Godfrey used a variety of techniques at the Gate as, for example, four simultaneous scenes in O'Neill's *Desire Under the Elms*, 1930–31, and moving pictures with the aid of a cine-kodak in Toller's expressionist *Hoppla*, 1929, a fore-runner of things to come.

Period Pastiche

These theatres were in revolt against the realism which still dominated the West End stage. This at its best was represented by the work of George Harris for Reandean. He was a designer of great facility and variety, best known for his settings for Flecker's *Hassan*, 1923, in which he used a white background reminiscent of *Sumurûn*. He set *Will Shakespeare* in decorated hessian curtains, which showed his tendency to adopt some elements of the new stagecraft.

Technological advances, such as the ability to black out the stage, enabled scenery to be changed without more than fractional waits. The objection to painted and built-up sets had been overcome. At the same time a taste arose for period flavours and neo-romantic styles.

Among the artists discovered by Cochran was Rex Whistler,[152] whose heart was in the Georgian and Regency and who could seize on the quintessence of a period, albeit

---

151. E.O.H. 'The Art of the Theatre—Mr. Norman Macdermott's Settings', *Studio*, 1919, Vol. 27, p. 65.
152. Cecil Beaton's appreciation in *The Masque*, 1947, with coloured illustrations.

with a quizzical eye. He did not overclutter his stage with detail but with subtle skill recreated visually the essence of the play's time. His wit echoed Wilde's when, in *The Ideal Husband*, 1943, he contrasted two ceremonial Georgian rooms, one in green, the other in blue, with the Victorian clutter in red of Lord Goring's Library. This may be compared with Cecil Beaton's splendid, if heavily upholstered, décor for *Lady Windermere's Fan*, 1945. Whistler also designed for ballet and opera. His evocation of the seamier side of 18th century life after Hogarth in *The Rake's Progress* may be contrasted with the delicate romanticism of his *Spectre de la Rose* and his Gothic ruin for *Les Sylphides*. By his death in the war England lost a scene designer with a unique flair for seeing past periods from a modern detached viewpoint.

Another of Cochran's protégés, Oliver Messel, had a similar gift for recreating a period, though he was more at home with the baroque and rococo and therefore with neo-classical, architectural themes. His quality of magic is well illustrated in the permanent scene of the conservatory for Anouilh's *Ring Round the Moon*, 1950, which had a shimmering insubstantiality according with the play's bitter-sweet fantasy. His *Idomeneo* set for Glyndebourne (Plate 62) is a good example of his recreation of a neo-classical style. One of his most ambitious mountings was for the ballet of *The Sleeping Princess* at Covent Garden, where sumptuous baroque scenery and costumes in beautiful colours represented all that was best in the revival of the painted scene.

A younger generation of scene painters worked in the same vein: among them Loudon Sainthill, who created a submarine coloured *Tempest* at Stratford, 1951, and whose *Pericles* succeeded in combining richness with symbolism.

Motley worked in many styles from unit sets to opulent décors. The unit set for *Hamlet*, Stratford, 1958 (Plate 65), depended on curtains for a change of scene but was richer in decoration than those of some other practitioners. In contrast, Leslie Hurry's scene for Helpmann's *Hamlet* ballet (Plate 64),

PLATE 62. Oliver Messel, *Idomeneo*. Glyndebourne.

with its painted perspectives, baroque architecture and decoration, and gigantic menacing figure, symbolises Hamlet's
nightmare by expressionist distortion. His restless, swirling
designs, streak of pure fantasy, and brilliant deep colouring,
were in evidence in his three versions of *Swan Lake*. On the
other hand for *The Ring*, Covent Garden, 1954, he used bare
Appia-like settings. Another great colourist who has worked
in the theatre is John Piper, whose romantic and unreal
designs have an architectural quality, as in those for Britten's
Rape of Lucrece (Plate 63). Particularly in opera, with its large
19th century repertory, and in classical ballet, romantic and
richly painted scenery with period flavour continues to
188   flourish.

PLATE 63. John Piper, Britten's opera *The Rape of Lucrece*.

The fashion for producing Shakespeare's plays in every conceivable period encouraged the employment of scene designers who could reproduce period settings. The claim that the universality of the plays would thus be demonstrated and a fresh approach to them revealed has often been proved false by the disturbing duality and inconsistency of words and setting.

With these efforts came a revival of older methods of staging. Oliver Messel designed *The Rivals*, 1945, with scene shifts in front of the audience, and more frequently than not the spectator now enters the theatre to see the set in place with no concealing curtain. *Much Ado* at Stratford in 1949 had scenery by Mariano Andreu which opened and shut, and

189

PLATE 64. Leslie Hurry, Helpmann's ballet, *Hamlet*.

even *periaktoi* have been employed by René Allio for the National Theatre's *Recruiting Officer*.

The post-war period was completely eclectic and every type of scenery was in use. Painted splendour existed side by side with austere, abstract and plastic settings. The old ways jostled with the new and audiences were ready to accept many different inventions to create stage illusion.

Post-war Innovations and Innovators
In the welter of styles today the trend is towards a frank recognition that the stage is theatrical and not realistic and this must be made evident in the mounting. The new move-

190

PLATE 65. Motley, *Hamlet*. Stratford-upon-Avon.

ment persuaded designers that they must create an art of the theatre to replace 19th century attempts to delude audiences into the feeling that they were actually looking at the place and time in which the play was set. The reaction against design as an element in theatrical unity has been mentioned under constructivism. It was also developed in the political theatre which arose in Germany between the wars. This made use of photographic projections and documentary films, both initiated by Erwin Piscator in 1924 and 1925 respectively. Brecht acclaimed these as transforming a dead background into a living presence. He had no use for artistic values in the settings for his plays; only for those functional pieces and methods which could forward his social purposes by objectify-

191

ing situations intellectually and so detaching audiences from emotional responses. He used any device to help get over his message; projected photographs, moving pictures, posters, all without reference to their artistic integration. The visit to London of his Berliner Ensemble in 1956 led some producers and designers to apply his theories in a wider field.

Joan Littlewood's production of *Oh! What a Lovely War* is a typical example of Brechtian influence. News bulletins were flashed on to the back scene; back projections of films or slides were thrown on to a screen. This multi-media technique is now an accepted convention which serves to counterpoint the text. The total abandonment of atmosphere which Brecht advocated was seen in Peter Brook's production of *Lear*, 1962, played in an unvarying white light which left storms and heath to the imagination.

The exposure of spots and lighting units is another way in which modern staging abjures the concealment of the means by which effects are wrought. Honesty is substituted for magic. The Mermaid Theatre had such lighting from its inception; theatre in the round has no choice.

Debates in the post-war theatre have concentrated on the best way of achieving audience-stage relationship and there have been many experiments to discover the ideal shape of a theatre. Audiences surrounding the stage; stages surrounding the audience, as in medieval times, and adaptable theatres which could be accommodated to four or five forms to suit various plays, have been tried. The proscenium has been eliminated or negated by thrust stages which penetrated into the audience. Tyrone Guthrie, in staging the 15th century *Three Estates*, Edinburgh Assembly Hall, 1949, showed how effective the thrust stage could be. Entrances and exits through the auditorium gangways brought the spectators into closer participation, as they had done with Poel and Reinhardt. This led to the erection of the first professional theatre in England with an open stage at Chichester in 1961, which was modelled on the festival theatre at Stratford, Ontario.

The first professional theatre-in-the-round was erected here by Stephen Joseph in Stoke-on-Trent after experiments in halls. None of these precluded scenery, though they modified it and compelled it to be architectural rather than pictorial. Peter Cheeseman has demonstrated that three types of scenery can be employed in theatre-in-the-round: firstly, levels can be built up all over the stage with access by ramps and stairs furnished with props to provide colour; secondly, scenic elements can be suspended above the acting area; thirdly, surfaces on peripheral stages or beyond the acting area, but within the sight lines, can be used for decorations. On the other hand, no scenery at all is needed for some productions.[153]

Flooring becomes of importance in structural settings. Stratford has had for some years false stages, either flat or raked, of metal or of wood, with antique patinas or carpets. John Bury, one of their designers, considers the stage floor the most important element in design[154] and he exhibited a large mosaic circle in *The Physicists* at the Aldwych. A tilted circular disc, first used as a symbol by Wieland Wagner in his revolutionary production of *The Ring* at Bayreuth, was used in a new staging at Covent Garden by Schneider-Siemessen, 1964. More recently a disc of brass and aluminium, designed by Kenneth Rowell, was seen in the Prospect Company's *Edward II* and *Richard II*. Its concentric circles were echoed by a curving forestage and fibreglass ramps leading to a gallery. The disc was raised on a base and an effect of floating was produced by a surrounding black out.[155]

The last decades are also remarkable for the new materials brought into use. As we have seen, metal was extensively employed. Bury erected tubular scaffolding at Stratford East, where he trained the hard way under Joan Littlewood,

153. *Tabs*, March 1971, Vol. 29.
154. Association of British Theatre Technicians, *News Letter*, Vol. 2, No. 2, p. 28.
155. *Tabs*, March 1970, Vol. 28, No. 1.

PLATE 66. John Bury, *Richard II*. Set model for Stratford-upon-Avon.

picking up raw materials from scrap heaps which he believed in using instead of synthetics. When commissioned to design the cycle of history plays for the Royal Shakespeare Theatre he created a metal setting with walls of copper treated to resemble steel (Plate 66). Its hard, glinting appearance symbolised the armoured wars and demonstrated the designer's belief that the setting should 'provide a sounding board for the actor's imagination' and 'supply him with the

194

basic imagery that he needs'.[156]

Even more widespread is the use of plastics such as polystyrene, perspex, fibreglass and latex rubber compounds. They are light to handle and, in the case of foam rubber, can be modelled on hard wood and sprayed to look like bronze or copper. Spraying on in gold or colour is extensively used both in scenery and costumes, and rough surfaces have been achieved by means of sawdust. Paint is now usually emulsion rather than distemper.

Sean Kenny, another of Joan Littlewood's protégés, has mounted several musicals and so brought modern styles and techniques into the most traditional of forms. He does not believe in a separate art of decoration. For *Oliver* he wished to convey Dickensian London as felt by the lost boy, and therefore dwarfed him in an outsize décor of winding stairways, beams and doorways on various planes.[157]

Ralph Koltai, who is one of our most experimental designers, has worked on both plays and operas, including two by Brecht. He aims to design an environment which springs from the text as interpreted by the director. The eye of the spectator, he says, should go first to the actor, then to his background, then back to actor. He stresses the modern idea that the setting, whether for Shakespeare, Wagner or Shaw, must be made expressive in terms of today.[158] His wall-less scene for *Major Barbara* was changed in view of the audience whilst music played. The all male *As You Like It* for the National Theatre he envisaged as a dream in which there was no reality—only a hint of timeless trees. Hanging tubes shimmered in the light creating great ground shadows (Plate 67). His sense of the cosmic found expression in the opening of *Back to Methuselah*, while the earth in an eclipse of the sun shrank to an apple as the actor appeared out of space. Again

156. *Times*, December 12, 1970, interview with Michael Billington.
157. Kenny, 'Designing Oliver', *Tabs*, September 1960, Vol. 18, No. 2, illustrated.
158. 'Conversation. Nicholas Georgiadis, Ralph Koltai', *Drama*, Winter, 1969, pp. 41–58; *Times*, January 23, 1971, interview with Alan Blyth.

PLATE 67. Ralph Koltai, *As You Like It*. Forest of Arden. National
Theatre production.

in *The Ring*, Coliseum, 1970–1971, Koltai suggested a planetary significance by a silver, fragmented globe. He adopted kinetic elements in a Rhine of moving blue tubes and a background of mirrors whose double image proved rather distracting. Koltai favours plastics for the light effects obtainable on them. One of the most abstract designers, he has transferred to the stage the optical, illusory effects of modern art.

The kinetic projections of the Czech designer, Svoboda, as seen in *Die Frau ohne Schatten* at Covent Garden, have influenced scenographers, as have the silver hanging cords of his *Three Sisters* at the National Theatre.

In this plastic-metallic age scene painting is only one method of mounting, but it is practised by British designers, such as Carl Toms and Georgiadis, and by foreign visitors, such as Visconti and Zeffirelli. Light painting and projection despite, it is not the end of the road, either for scene painting or perspective. Our period is one of infinite variety.

The history of scene painting is the history of an illusion. The kind of illusion is controlled by the taste of the time and by the entertainments which the time favours. So we have seen a progress from the baroque ideal world through the expression of the romantic spirit to the desire to illustrate in canvas and paint the actual environment; from the reaction from this to symbolic and abstract settings and scenery for art's sake to the eclecticism of today. Audiences are now conditioned to accept any form of illusion or dis-illusion, even to the occasional total abolition of setting. To all this Britain has made many outstanding contributions—notably in the open form of the Elizabethan stage, in masque and romantic scenery, in the spectacles of Charles Kean and of the Victorian pantomime, and in the revolutionary ideas of Craig.

Selected Book List

General

Altman, George; Freud, Ralph; Macgowan, Kenneth; Melnitz, Wilhelm, *Theatre Pictorial*, 1953.
History of World Theatre recorded in illustrations with explanatory text.

Beaumont, Cyril W., *Five Centuries of Ballet Design*, n.d.
Illustrations of history of ballet with an introduction.

Gascoigne, Bamber, *World Theatre*, 1968.
Comparative scenic designs are excellently illustrated with many unusual examples. Includes oriental theatre.

Laver, James, *Drama, its Costume and Décor*, 1951.
Illustrated; good introduction to the subject with international coverage and a bibliography.

Merchant, W. Moelwyn, *Shakespeare and the Artist*, 1959.
Illustrated; covers Shakespearean productions as well as Shakespeare in art.

Nicoll, Allardyce, *The Development of the Theatre*, 1927; reprinted, 1966.
Illustrated; essential for comparison of English with foreign scenography.

Odell, George C. D., *Shakespeare from Betterton to Irving*, 1920; reprinted, 1963.
Illustrated; excellent sections on scenery and staging for each period.

Simonson, Lee, *The Art of Scenic Design*, 1950.
A well illustrated book by an American scene designer. Covers European and American designs from Serlio to mid-20th century. Brief introductory survey.

Southern, Richard, *Changeable Scenery*, 1952.
  Illustrated; the best and fullest account of the technique of scene changes, with particular reference to the English groove method.

Medieval and Elizabethan

Hodges, C. Walter, *The Globe Restored: A Study of the Elizabethan Theatre*, 1953; revised, 1968.
  Illustrated; the sanest account of the subject.

Kernodle, George, *From Art to Theatre*, 1943.
  Illustrated; a pioneering work on the influence of the street theatre on the stage.

Lawrence, W. J., *The Elizabethan Playhouse and Other Studies*, 2, [1913].
  Illustrated. See 'The Origin of the English Picture Stage'.

——, *Pre-Restoration Stage Studies*, 1929.
  See 'Elizabethan Stage Realism'; 'Characteristics of Platform Stage Spectacle'.

Nicoll, Allardyce, *Masks, Mimes and Miracles*, 1931.
  Illustrated; valuable chapters on the secular and religious drama of the middle ages.

Reynolds, George F., *The Staging of Elizabethan Plays at the Red Bull*, 1940.

Southern, Richard, *The Medieval Theatre in the Round*, 1957.
  Illustrated; a detailed consideration of the staging of *The Castle of Perseverance* and related matters.

Wickham, Glynne, *Early English Stages, 1300–1660*, Vol. 1, 1959; Vol. 2, 1963.
  Illustrated; several chapters on staging, including street theatres and tournaments.

Inigo Jones

Campbell, Lily B., *Scenes and Machines on the English Stage during the Renaissance*, 1923; reprinted, 1960.
  Illustrated; concerned with classical influences on Renaissance theatre, staging and perspective scenery. An account

199

of the work of Inigo Jones and Webb and a short section on the Restoration.

Designs by Inigo Jones for Masques and Plays at Court, ed. Percy Simpson and C. F. Bell. Walpole and Malone Societies, 1934, Vol. 12.

The only annotated and illustrated catalogue of all the masque designs by Jones at Chatsworth. It is the basis of their attributions to various masques.

Lawrence, W. J., *The Elizabethan Playhouse and Other Studies*, 1912.

Illustrated. See 'The Mounting of the Carolan Masques'.

Nicoll, Allardyce, *Stuart Masques and the Renaissance Stage*, 1937. Illustrated; a comprehensive study of the staging of the masques with reference to Italian theatre practice.

Southern, Richard, 'Observations on Lansdowne Ms. No. 1171', *Theatre Notebook*, October 1947, Vol. 2, pp. 6-19.

Full account of the staging of *Salmacida Spolia*.

Strong, Roy, *Festival Designs by Inigo Jones. An Exhibition of Drawings for Scenery and Costumes for the Court Masques of James I and Charles I*, 1967–1968.

Illustrated.

Caroline Stage and Davenant Operas

Bentley, G. E., *The Jacobean and Caroline Stage*, 1941–1968, 6 Vols.

The standard work on the theatre of the period.

Keith, W. G., 'Designs for the First Movable Scenery on the English Public Stage', *Burlington Magazine*, April 1914, Vol. 25.

Richards, Kenneth, 'Changeable Scenery for Plays on the Caroline Stage', *Theatre Notebook*, October 1968, Vol. 23, pp. 6–20.

Restoration

Boswell, Eleanore, *The Restoration Court Stage (1600–1702)*, 1932; reprinted, 1966.

Illustrated; a detailed account of productions, including that of *Calisto*, from state records which provide much information on methods of staging.

Jackson, Allen, 'Restoration Scenery, 1656–1680', *Restoration and 18th Century Research*, November 1964, Vol. 3, No. 2.

Summers, Montague, *The Restoration Theatre*, 1934.
Illustrated; chapters on scenery, costumes and curtains.

Georgian Theatre

Burnim, Kalman, *David Garrick: Director*, 1961.
Contains much information about the scenery of his presentations.

Croft-Murray, Edward, *John Devoto, A Baroque Scene Painter*, 1953.
Illustrated; Society for Theatre Research.

Rosenfeld, S.; Croft-Murray, E., 'Checklist of Scene Painters working in Great Britain and Ireland in the 18th Century', *Theatre Notebook*, 1964–1966, Vols. 19, 20.

Rosenfeld, S., 'A Georgian Scene-Painter at Work', *British Museum Quarterly*, Vol. 34, Nos. 1–2.
The painter is Michael Angelo Rooker.

Thomas, Russell, 'Stage Decorations of London Theatres, 1700–1800', *Modern Philology*, November 1944, Vol. 42, No. 2, pp. 65–78.

Romantic Movement

Allen, Ralph G., 'The Wonders of Derbyshire', *Theatre Survey*, 1961, Vol. 2, pp. 54–66.

——, De Loutherbourg and Captain Cook', *Theatre Research*, 1962, Vol. 4, No. 3, pp. 195–221.

——, 'The Eidophusikon', *Theatre Design and Technology*, December 1966, Vol. 77, pp. 12–16.

——, 'Capon's Scenes for Melodrama', *Theatre Research*, 1966, Vol. 8, No. 1.

Donohue, J. W., 'Kemble's Production of *Macbeth*', *Theatre Notebook*, January 1967, Vol. 21, pp. 63–74.

Lawrence, W. J., 'The Pioneers of Modern Stage Mounting. Phillipe Jacques de Loutherbourg, R.A.', *Magazine of Art*, 1895, pp. 172–177.

——, 'William Capon', *ibid.*, p. 289.

Oliver, Anthony, and Saunders, John, 'De Loutherbourg and *Pizarro* 1799', *Theatre Notebook*, October 1965, Vol. 20, p. 30.

Pyne, W. H., *Wine and Walnuts*, Vol. 1, pp. 281–304.

A contemporary account of De Loutherbourg's work.

Rosenfeld, S., 'The Eidophusikon Illustrated', *Theatre Notebook*, December 1963, Vol. 18, p. 52.

——, 'Scene Designs of William Capon', *Theatre Notebook*, 1956, Vol. 10, p. 118.

Victorian Theatre

Emanuel, Frank L., 'William Roxby Beverley', *Walkers Quarterly*, January 1921, Vol. 2.

Fitzgerald, Percy, *The World Behind the Scenes*, 1881.

Part 1, 'Stage Illusions—Mechanism'; Part 2, 'Spectacles, Feeries, &c.'.

Particularly useful for descriptions of how effects were managed in the late Victorian theatre. Comparisons with French and German counterparts.

Harker, Joseph, *Studio and Stage*, 1924.

A scene painter's reminiscences and views.

Hewitt, Barnard, *History of the Theatre from 1800 to the present*, 1970.

Illustrated; a good survey with international coverage.

Lloyds, Frederick, *Practical Guide to Scene Painting and Painting in Distemper*, [1875].

A manual by one of Charles Kean's painters.

Macready, W. C., *William Charles Macready's 'King John'*, ed. Charles Shattuck, 1962.

A facsimile promptbook with reproductions of Telbin's designs.

——, *Mr. Macready Produces 'As You Like It' ; A Prompt-Book*

Study, ed. Charles Shattuck, 1962.

Reynolds, Ernest, *Early Victorian Drama (1830–1870)*, 1936. Mainly critical, but sections on scenery, machinery, costume and lighting.

Rowell, George, *The Victorian Theatre*, 1956. Illustrated; general survey up to 1914 with good sections on scenery, machinery, lighting and a valuable bibliography.

Southern, R., 'The Picture-Frame Proscenium of 1880', *Theatre Notebook*, April 1951, Vol. 5, pp. 59–61.

Strange, Edward F., 'The Scenery of Charles Kean's Plays and the Great Scene-Painters of his Day', *Magazine of Art*, 1902, Vol. 24, pp. 455–459.

Telbin, William [L.], 'Act Drops', *Magazine of Art*, 1895–1896, Vol. 18, p. 335.

——, 'Art in the Theatre', *Magazine of Art*, 1899, Vol. 12, pp. 42–47; pp. 195–201.

Waitzkin, Leo, *The Witch of Wych Street*, 1933. A study of Madame Vestris.

Watson, Ernest Bradlee, *Sheridan to Robertson*, 1926. Much information about staging. Particularly valuable for the section on Vestris, the importance of whose realistic innovations he was the first to appreciate.

The New Stagecraft and the Modern Theatre

Appia, Adolphe, catalogue of the exhibition at the Victoria and Albert Museum, 1970. Illustrated; with articles on Appia and Wagner, Dalcroze, Gluck, and Appia and the Drama.

Bablet, Denis, 'Edward Gordon Craig and Scenography', *Theatre Research*, 1971, Vol. 11, No. 1, pp. 7–22.

Beaumont, Cyril W., *Design for the Ballet*, n.d. Illustrations of ballet designs from 1890 to 1937 with an introduction.

Carter, Huntly, *The New Spirit in Drama and Art*, 1912.

——, *The New Spirit in the European Theatre, 1914–1924*, 1925.

Cheney, Sheldon, *Stage Decoration*, 1928.

Valuable for its consideration of theories of staging which led up to the revolution of Craig and Appia. He limits his approval to this type of staging.

Craig, Edward, *Gordon Craig*, 1968.

Illustrated; the outstanding biography by his son with full accounts of his theories and staging practices.

——, 'Gordon Craig and Hubert von Herkomer', *Theatre Research*, 1969, Vol. 10, No. 1, pp. 7–16.

Craig, Edward Gordon, *On the Art of the Theatre*, 1911, reprinted with a new preface, 1925.

Illustrated.

——, *Scene*, 1923.

Designs illustrating his theories with an introduction.

Design in the Theatre, ed. Geoffrey Holme. Commentary by George Sheringham and James Laver, *Studio*, 1927.

Illustrated; contributions by Craig, Cochran and Playfair.

Fletcher, Ifan Kyrle, 'Charles Ricketts and the Theatre', *Theatre Notebook*, October 1967, Vol. 22, pp. 6–23.

Fuerst, W. R., and Hume, S. J., *Twentieth Century Stage Decoration*, 1928.

Illustrated.

Hainaux, René, *Stage Design Throughout the World since 1935*, [1956].

Illustrated.

——, *Stage Design Throughout the World since 1950*, 1964.

Illustrated.

Harbin, Billy J., 'Cambridge Festival Theatre, 1926–1933', *American Educational Theatre Journal*, December 1969, pp. 392–402.

Leeper, Janet, *Edward Gordon Craig*, 1948.

Illustrated.

Messel, Oliver, *Stage Designs and Costumes*, 1933.

Illustrated.

Moderwell, Hiram Kelly, *The Theatre of To-day*, 1927.

Nash, George, *Edward Gordon Craig, 1872–1966*, 1967.

Illustrated; catalogue of exhibition at the Victoria and Albert

Museum.

Rowell, Kenneth, *Stage Design*, 1968.

Illustrated; a stage designer discusses the various international styles and techniques employed today and their development from the end of the 19th century.

Speaight, Robert, *William Poel and the Elizabethan Revival*, 1954. Society for Theatre Research.

The only full account.

Warre, Michael, *Designing and Making Scenery*, 1966.

Illustrated; a practical manual by a practising scene designer.

Woodruff, Graham, 'Terence Gray and Theatre Design', *Theatre Research*, 1971, Vol. 9, pp. 114–132.

Index